The Blame Game

The Complete Guide to Blaming:

How to Play and How to Quit

What others are saying about The Blame Game...

"Rather than blaming, start reading! This is a thoughtful, accessible book that could actually make you happier."
    -**Tal Ben-Shahar, PhD,** author of *Happier: Learn the Secrets to Daily Joy and Lasting Fulfillment*

"The Blame Game helps to usher in our new era of responsibility with: Ask not where the buck stops. It stops with thee."
    -**Tad Waddington, PhD,** author of *Lasting Contribution: How to Think, Plan, and Act to Accomplish Meaningful Work*

"Dr. Farber paints a persuasive picture of how ordinary is our extraordinary tendency to blame. More important, he shows how well-being will follow when we give it up."
    -**Ellen Langer, PhD,** author of *Counterclockwise: Mindful Health and the Power of Possibility*

"The Blame Game presents a humorous guide to blaming with practical and insightful ways to jump off the Blame Train. Dr. Farber's witty and informative style makes this a fun and edifying read. Take it seriously and it will change your life for the better."
    -**Jon Gordon,** author of *The Energy Bus* and *The No Complaining Rule: Positive Ways to Deal with Negativity at Work*

"If you are like me, you spend way too much time and energy blaming others for disappointments and offenses when you could be moving on with a productive and happy life. Want to learn how to stop blaming and live more abundantly? This is the book for you. Entertaining, yet thoughtful, playing the Blame Game will unclutter your emotions and your life."
    -**Everett L. Worthington Jr., PhD,** author of *Forgiving and Reconciling: Bridges to Wholeness and Hope*

"Throughout my career, supplementing my life experiences with thoughtful texts on management, psychology and human behavior have been invaluable. One of the difficulties with many of these is that it often feels like studying to digest the comments. This book effortlessly brings wit and readability to a vitally important topic no matter what rung of the ladder you are on and regardless of your field of interest. This text has the potential to transform individual lives and corporate cultures. I have placed it on my shelf of must read books!"
    -Joseph Kerschner, MD, Dean Medical College of Wisconsin, Professor, Otolaryngology, Medical College of Wisconsin

"To blame is human; to write about it with humor, skill, and insight is to write a book worth reading. How wonderful to have a help book that actually helps."
    -Herzl R. Spiro MD, PhD, Emeritus Professor of Psychiatry, The University of Wisconsin-Madison

"In a book that is long overdue, Dr. Farber identifies a critical problem most of us face: an unwillingness to hold ourselves accountable. While many of us seem to be all too willing to point fingers at others for our failings, Dr. Farber provides a map with which we can become more self-aware and, in the process, lead a more fulfilling life."
    -Ed Levitus, PhD, Associate Professor, Sheldon B. Lubar School of Business

"This book, written in a lighthearted, easy to read, conversational manner, is an eye opener. Blaming is everywhere. It drains our energy and focus and distracts us from getting to solutions. This book brings this fact to the forefront of our awareness, where it can be dealt with. Dr. Farber draws upon his own life experience so much so that, once finished, you feel as if you just had a long conversation with a good friend about something that really matters."
    -Peter Bandettini, PhD, Editor-in-Chief of NeuroImage, Director fMRI facility, National Institute of Mental Health

The Blame Game

The Complete Guide to Blaming:

How to Play and How to Quit

Neil E. Farber M.D., Ph.D.

DYNAMIC PUBLISHING GROUP
MEQUON, WI

Other books by Dr. Farber

Making Lemonade: 101 Recipes to Convert Negatives into Positives. Dynamic Publishing Group, WI. 2012.

The No Blaming Zone: An allegorically true story about creating positive changes, harnessing energy, and achieving potential through the simple act of taking responsibility. Dynamic Publishing Group, WI. 2015.

The Financial Industry's Guide to the No Blaming Zone. Dynamic Publishing Group, WI. 2015.

Check out Dr. Farber's Blame Game blog on PsychologyToday.com

Like us on Facebook: facebook.com/TheActionBoard

Check out TheKeytoAchieve.com to help establish and achieve your goals and your potential best you.

Contact: Neil@DHWI.net or TheKeytoAchieve@gmail.com

Copyright ©2008, 2010 by Neil E. Farber, MD, PhD, FAAP

Dynamic
Publishing Group

Mequon, WI
www.DHWI.net

All rights reserved. No part of this publication may be reproduced, stored in a retrieval system, or transmitted, in any form or by any means, electronic, mechanical, photocopying, recording or otherwise, without the prior written permission of the author.
Limit of Liability/Disclaimer of Warranty: While the publisher and author have used their best efforts in preparing this book, they make no representations or warranties with respect to the accuracy or completeness of the contents of this book and specifically disclaim any implied warranties of merchantability or fitness for a particular purpose. The advice and strategies contained herein may not be suitable for your situation. You should consult with a professional where appropriate. Neither the publisher nor author shall be liable for any loss of profit or any other commercial damages, including but not limited to special, incidental, consequential, or other damages.

ISBN-10: 0985302437
ISBN-13: 978-0-9853024-3-6
LCCN: 2010908052

Cover design by James Arneson

1st *edition: 2010. Bascom Hill Publishing Group*
2nd *edition: 2015. Dynamic Publishing Group*

Printed in the United States of America

Contents

Preface: Who's to blame for this book?................ xiii

Definition..xvii

Chapters

1. What is The Blame Game?...........................**1**
   What is the game?... 1
   When did it start?... 2
   Who bought the game?.. 6
   Who can play?... 6
   What are the rules of the game?........................... 9
   When will the game end?....................................... 10

2. Some Blaming Formats................................**12**
   Group blaming... 12
   Blaming in the Media.. 20
   Legal blaming... 29

3. Learning to Blame..**35**
   Inborn or learned behavior?................................... 35
   As children.. 36
   Learning from siblings... 39
   Learning from friends.. 41

4. Why We Blame..**45**
   Innate need... 46
   Copying behavior... 46
   Avoid responsibility... 47
   Internalize vs. externalize....................................... 51
   Wrong focus.. 52
   It's easier... 54
   Afraid of Success.. 56
   Programmed to accept the negative......................58

5. **How We Blame**..61
   - *Unintentionally*..62
   - *Subtly*..65
   - *Blatantly*...66
   - *Casually*..67
   - *Secretly*...68
   - *Deceitfully*..70

6. **Who We Blame**...74
   - *Ourselves*..74
   - *Family*...76
   - *Friends*..77
   - *Spouses*..78
   - *Bosses and co-workers*..79
   - *Teachers and students*..81
   - *Strangers*..84

7. **What We Blame**..86
   - *God*..87
   - *Satan*...93
   - *Nature*...93
   - *Genetics*..96
   - *Other (Cars, Animals, Holidays, etc)*.............................101

8. **Governmental Blame**.....................................111
   - *Elections*...111
   - *National Debt*..115
   - *Security*..117
   - *Obamacare*..117
   - *Internal Revenue Service*...118
   - *Privacy Violations*...119
   - *Entitlements*..119

9. Problems With The Game. 122
Not fun…especially for the blamee 122
It's expensive 123
You could be wrong 124
Hinders relationships 126
Relies on negativity 126

10. Benefits of Quitting. 128
More control of your life 128
Better mental health 130
Achieve your potential 131
Enhance relationships 132
Improve your marriage 132
Make new friends 133
Greater success in business 133
Gain respect 134
Better physical health 135

11. How To Stop Playing. 137
Acknowledge that you have control 138
Take responsibility 140
Realize that failures are steps to success 141
Judge favorably 142
Empathize – externalize for others 144
Make excuses for others 145
Explain, don't complain 148
Believe in something 150
A coincidence? 155

12. Conclusions. 159

Dedication

This book is dedicated to those who brought me here—my mother, Linda, and my late father, Michael; and those who will carry me through—my children Kaelah, Shoshana, and Sarena. I thank you and love you all.

Preface: Who's to blame for this book?

It's not my fault! If you don't like the name of this book or its content, it's not my fault! While this book was indeed written by me, I am the product of both my genetic pool and my environment. Therefore, there are many others that should at least share the responsibility for this book.

Let's start with the list of candidates. In terms of heredity, I am not just the result of genes from my mother and father. Nor did it start with my great-grandparents, although they obviously must take on at least part of the responsibility. I learned in medical school that my genetic makeup stems from way, way back. In fact, Jewish tradition has it that there are three Jewish "tribes"— Kohen, Levite, and Israelite. Kohens (Cohens) and Levites are direct descendants of Aaron (Moses' brother) and the line has been passed from father to son for more than 3,300 years. Drs. Skorecki and Hammer have demonstrated that there are common genetic markers on the Y chromosome of DNA, known as the Cohen Modal Haplotype (CMH), which proves that there is indeed a common ancestor for all of those Cohens and Levites (which includes me). So I can at least recruit the biblical figures of Aaron and Moses to share in some responsibility for all the things that I do— both good and bad. It gives me a warm feeling knowing that when I screw up something, I can blame it on Moses! Am I implying that this whole thing began with Moses? Of course not, this path of blame far predates Moses. Whether you believe in the Big Bang or a Creator, we were all derived from some common ancestors, without whom, I would not be here and there would be no book. Thus, what might be termed "initial blame" can be attributed to these ancient relatives. Basically, none of my familial lineage is able to side-step any responsibility when it comes to my actions. Although my great-grandfathers were very religious, spiritual and righteous men, this does not excuse them for helping create my genetic identity. They are all at fault!

Okay, enough about my family. How about my upbringing? I was born in Toronto, Canada, in the '60s as the firstborn son of Linda and Michael Farber. Negating the above genetic arguments, I was unwittingly influenced by both my parents from the time I was a newborn. My mother is a teacher and an artist. She taught me how to read and write. She encouraged my creativity and the use of the right side of my brain. My father was brilliant and more strict and linear. He was a pharmacist, businessman, and contractor. He taught me the importance of hard work, and how to focus on left brain activities, such as Jewish genetic markers. Obviously, these two bear much responsibility for anything that I do. As an aside, my mother is still relatively surprised that I'm writing this book as one of the few middle class Jewish authors who is not also Buddhist.

I have two biologic siblings and one adopted sister. I don't have to tell anyone growing up with brothers and sisters that they can't help but influence how you view the world. Learning to share, learning to not share, learning to fight, learning to make up, and learning for the first time to stand up for what you believe. My brother and sisters carry most of the responsibility for this. However, realistically speaking, my siblings did not act alone to influence me in not-so-subtle positive and negative ways, which through a long string of events led me to write down all this stuff. I have had several dozen teachers, ranging from bad to amazing, in grade school, junior high school, high school, university, medical school, graduate school, medical internship, anesthesiology residency, and pediatric fellowship. Each of these teachers had teachers and professors who, in turn, taught them; as well as school administrators who influenced how and what they taught. There were also government officials and elected representatives who set up rules and guidelines for the schools. They each must embrace some ultimate responsibility for my actions. Training in martial arts and self-defense for almost forty years has influenced many of my thoughts, feelings, and actions regarding all facets of my life. There have been many incredible instructors who have "shown me the way" and essentially acted as my life coaches. As I freely give these masters credit for many of my successes, they should also have to take the fall for my failures. The list of instructors includes: Grandmasters John Pellegrini, Avi Nardia, Miki Erez, Maurice Elmalem, Don (The Dragon) Wilson, Moti Horenstein, Dana Abbott, Cynthia (Lady Dragon) Rothrock, Bill (Superfoot) Wallace, Chuck Norris, Chaim Peer, Chaim Bachar, Moni Isaac, Cary-Hiroyuki Tagawa, Dennis Hannover and Park Sang Young and Masters Mark Gridley, David Rivas, Paul Chay, and Greg Chay. It should go without saying that the masters who trained my masters should not be excluded from taking some of the blame that you might otherwise dole out to me.

I acknowledge some very important people in my life who have acted as mentors and spiritual guides either directly and in person or through their writings. These individuals are too numerous to mention them all by name. However, Rabbis David Aaron, David Cooper, Harold Kushner, Marc Berkson, Dovid, Menachem, and Moti Rappaport, Moshe Spalter, Lawrence Kushner, Joseph Telushkin, Herbert Feder, and Jacob Herber, have been wonderfully important influences in my life.

Other amazing writers and gurus who I must acknowledge and thank are Ram Dass, Yehudis Samet, Richard Carlson, Eckhart Tolle, Yitta Halberstam, David Pollay, Jon Gordon, Judith Leventhal, Jack Canfield, Dan Millman, Thich Nhat Hanh, and His Holiness, The Dalai Lama as well as Drs. Steven Covey, Tal Ben Shahar, Deepak Chopra, Martin Seligman, G. Lynn Nelson, Ellen Langer, Ed Diener, Everett Worthington, Michael McCullough, Robert Enright, Barbara Fredrickson, Chris Peterson, and Jon Kabat-Zinn. I am eternally grateful for their guidance and wisdom. Much of what I write is based on their teachings. Thus, I also want to assign a good proportion of the blame and responsibility toward them. It would be a grave error for me not to thank (blame) my mentors in medicine who are too numerous to name, but a few of them include Drs. Joseph Kerschner, David Warltier, George Hoffman, Garrett Gross, Robert Holzman, Steven Butz, Richard Berens,

Thomas Sato, Steven Weisman, Todd Troshynski, and Peter Bandettini, Gail Randel, and Mary Ann Vann.

We learn something from everyone. My children have each taught me many valuable lessons. They should also be blamed for my words and actions, but do it gently, I love them dearly. I have been a teacher for many years and have taken care of thousands of patients, including many in foreign countries on medical missions. I have taught in psychology, positivity, parenting, ethics, pharmacology, martial arts, medicine, mysticism, and meditation. For years, my students and patients have been my best teachers. I am blessed when able to interact with students and patients; I am able to grow and learn from each of them. In other words, none of them can escape the inevitable blame that you have the right to mete out for this work. I would also be shirking my responsibility if I did not allocate much liability and blame for this finished project to my dear friends Mark Gridley and Rhonda Devorkin, for their helpful critiques and suggestions, without which I would not have completed this book and subjected you to its messages. Finally, it is you dear reader, who has begged, stole, borrowed or perhaps even purchased this book. Without your active role, there would be no need for me to apologize. So, I can state with clarity and strength that you are at least, in part, to blame.

While I tried to be complete in my list of accomplices, I may have missed someone who would alleviate some of my accountability and share with me in the blame for this book. If so, I would like to apologize, but I was distracted by something on the radio. So... it's not my fault!

This second edition of The Blame Game corrects some erroneous errors (created by the first publisher), of course, and adds some more current events to the list of examples upon who and what to blame. Several of the examples have come from readers who have contributed to my Blame Game blog on PsychologyToday.com. If you have some great examples of blaming in our society, please send me a message and if I include it in the next edition, I can blame you too.

Definition

You may be well-experienced at blaming and just need a refresher course or you may be a novice. You may be an old pro at blaming or perhaps you've never tried it before but have always thought about getting involved either as a hobby or as a profession. Here are some definitions for the term *BLAME:*

- To censure.
- To express disapprobation for something wrong.
- Imputation of fault to charge or accuse.
- To bring reproach upon.
- To blemish.
- Culpability.
- To hurt.
- Slander or defame.
- To chide, scold, rebuke, or discredit.

Neil Farber M.D., Ph.D.

1. What is The Blame Game?

"The man who can smile when things go wrong has thought of someone else he can blame it on."

Robert Bloch

The Blame Game is one of the most popular games ever invented. We all play it some time in our lives. But what do you really know about the Game? How long has it been around? Who started it? Who can buy the Game and who can play it? What exactly are the rules of the Game and when does it officially end? This chapter is the background for some of the other concepts found later in the book. If you do decide to skip it and later get lost in terminology, don't blame me! Now, let's get started.

What is The Game?

He runs, arm outstretched, index finger pointed toward a stranger, yelling, "It was him, it was him, he did it!" He blames—he scores! The Blame Game is a fascinating competition in which the participants try intensely to find fault in others. After pronouncing liability, through several techniques such as the "responsibility shift," the blamers falsely receive self-accolades. Like golf, bowling, poker, and pool, there is much debate whether blaming should be technically considered a "sport." London has applied and received the honor to host the summer Olympics in 2012. The International Blaming Federation (IBF) has made a convincing case to the International Olympic Committee (IOC) for the inclusion of "Blaming" in the Olympics. In order to be in included on the Summer Olympics program, it must be widely practiced by men in at least seventy-five countries on four continents, and by women in at least forty countries on three continents. No problem.

When did it start?

The *Guinness Book of World Records* has awarded *Blaming* the title of the world's "Oldest Game." Although rarely publicized, the Blame Game has been played since the beginning of recorded time. The first successful blaming was performed shortly after the creation of the world, according to the Judeo-Christian-Muslim view.

Adam and Eve were the first man and woman created by God according to the Bible and the Qur'an. This story is told in the book of *Genesis*. God creates Adam from the dust of the earth, and subsequently Eve, from Adam's side. God tells them that they can have anything they want, except to eat or even touch the forbidden fruit from the Tree of the Knowledge of Good and Evil or they will die (John Milton described the fruit as an apple in his *Paradise Lost* novel in the 1600s, but that's not in the Bible). A serpent tells Eve that eating the forbidden fruit won't actually kill her. Eve explains to the serpent that God said that she shouldn't do it, and then Eve goes ahead and does it anyway. Then Eve, in turn, gives the fruit to Adam who, being of sound mind and body and with informed consent of what it was and the potential risks involved, also partakes of the fruit.

God is upset about Adam and Eve hiding themselves because of their nakedness, and asks rhetorically, "Who told thee that thou wast naked? Hast thou eaten of the tree, whereof I commanded thee that thou shouldest not eat?" Adam responds with the "Original Blame." "The woman whom Thou gavest to be with me, she gave me of the tree, and I did eat." It wasn't just a blame, it was a double-inclusive blame (worth more points). Adam blamed Eve for giving him the fruit, as if he was drugged with mind-altering poppies, tied to a Tree of Life and force-fed with pureed fruit. He also cleverly reminded God that it was God who gave him the woman in the first place. Thus, he argues, the initial blame and ultimate responsibility lies with God. God then turns to Eve and asks for her explanation of the events that transpired. Eve doesn't say, "I ate the fruit." Instead, she exclaims, "The serpent duped me, and I ate it." God didn't buy these excuses or accept the blame.

Having lost their jobs, Adam and Eve had to leave Eden and seek alternative career paths. Adam is cursed to labor and the woman is cursed to submit to her husband and to bear children in pain (until the introduction of epidurals). Thus, we can blame Adam every morning on our way out the door to the office, and women in labor can blame Eve.

The tradition of blaming was subsequently passed on to Adam and Eve's kids. Cain worked the land and Abel cared for the sheep; Abel's sacrifices and offerings were more favorable to God. Instead of looking at diverse forms of sacrificial offerings, seeking counseling, or trying to improve his self-worth, Cain blamed Abel for his troubles and killed him. Like his parents, unsuccessful in the Blame Game, Cain is also punished and forced to wander the earth.

Bruce Feiler has written a book titled, *Abraham* about the man that many consider the father of the Jewish, Christian, and Muslim faiths. There is a Midrash (early Rabbinic story) that is similar to a story in the Qur'an that tells of a young Abraham employed in his father's store, whose merchandise consists primarily of idols for pagan worship. While his father is away, Abraham smashes all of the idols except the largest, and places the axe in its hands. When his father returns, Abraham blames the destruction on the idol. As Abraham knows how the idols were destroyed, his blaming was for the sake of his father's education. When his father says the idols are merely clay, Abraham uses this point to claim that there must be something more powerful then these idols.

Many years later, when Abraham was a spry one hundred years old he had a son named Isaac. When Isaac was nearing the end of his life and blind, he was to bestow his greatest blessings to his firstborn son, Esau. Esau had a twin brother, named Jacob, and in a moment of hunger and weakness, Esau sold his birthright to Jacob in exchange for some of his homemade Lentil soup (that must have been some soup). Jacob then goes to his father and pretends to be Esau. His father buys the ruse and gives the blessing. Upon finding this out, Esau exclaims, "he hath supplanted me these two times:

he took away my birthright; and, behold, now he hath taken away my blessing." He blamed his brother for his own indiscretion and vowed to slay Jacob. After many years of separation, Esau calmed down and forgave his brother.

Years later Jacob has twelve sons (and a daughter). Joseph, the second youngest, walks around wearing a very cool-looking colored coat that he received from his dad. Jacob did what parents shouldn't do; he played favorites. No one else got a really cool coat. They didn't even get a scarf or a pair of galoshes. Rather than having a family meeting or open discussion time with dad to work this out, the brothers blamed Joseph (first example of group blame) for their lack of colored coats and for not being the favorite. Joseph also told them of his dreams suggesting that he would rule over them. His brothers then blamed him for having these dreams. They were going to kill Joseph, and then decided to sell him into slavery instead. Years later, living in Egypt, Joseph's dreams had come true. His brothers were forced to pay him respect and ask his forgiveness. Had they not been so blinded with blame in the first place, they never would have been in that position.

There are thousands more biblical stories that clearly demonstrate that our forbearers were not above blaming parents, siblings, offspring, or anyone else who might come along. While Jews, Christians, and Muslims have traditionally understood Adam and Eve to have been real, historical figures, the science of human evolution does not always support that understanding. However, in a similar fashion to Adam and Eve, biologists have theorized that all living human beings have evolved from a matrilineal ancestor, known as Mitochondrial Eve, and a patrilineal ancestor, known as Y-chromosomal Adam. If you don't believe in Adam and Eve, there are interesting blaming stories involving uncouth prehistoric Neanderthals (sorry Geico® cavemen), which I was lucky enough to find in an old book called, *One Caveman's Story*. The book was written in pictographs and petroglyphs, since there was no ancient written language with a pronounceable alphabet until 3,000 BCE, so I paraphrase.

There was a fellow named Emalb who had been chasing some kind of large beast for over one thousand moons. He chased this animal through forests and over glaciers; around mountains and across large bodies of water. Emalb was obsessed with killing this animal. After losing the creature's trail for several suns, Emalb wandered into a neighboring village where his best Neanderthal friend lived and was shocked and dismayed at what he saw. His best friend Tluaf was sitting with his family enjoying a roast beast meal. It was *his* beast, the beast that Emalb had so painstakingly pursued for so long. He couldn't understand why his so-called friend had done this and blamed Tluaf and his family until the next ice age. Emalb never realized that the animal had actually died from old age outside of Tluaf's cave. Emalb's blame was so fierce that he went back to his village and spread the word that Tluaf's village had stolen "his beast." With his entire village blaming the neighboring village for this loss, they immediately went to war. There was much devastation, and had they known how to make fire, I'm sure things would have been burned as well as pillaged.

In prehistoric times, the cause of natural disasters was largely unknown. When bad things happened, the cavemen would look to something familiar to accuse. There are several examples listed suggesting that blame was typically placed on the shoulders of the weaker and slower members of the clan. When volcanoes would erupt, snow would start falling, lightening would strike, ice ages would appear, billion-pound ice ledges would fall into your supper, dinosaurs would eat all the children, or important elders would die, a member of the clan would shout out the name of someone who they thought should incur blame. The rest of the clan would take a vote. The guilty party would be fed to the wolves or banished from the rest of the group. If three or more cavemen shouted out the same name at the same time, they didn't need to vote; they took that as a sign of incredibly strong blame power and initiated sentencing.

Whether you believe in the Bible or believe in evolutionary theory, or both, there is an abundance of evidence that strongly suggests that blaming has been around for as long as man has been on this earth—if not longer. That something has stood the test of time doesn't make it right! Blaming others hurts us more than them. And when I say "us," I mean all of us. I will do my best to try to show you why I think there are problems with the Blame Game and the benefits of quitting the game.

Who bought The Game?

We all bought the game. We purchased the online, extended version and have been playing it non-stop since it arrived. We have been fooled into thinking that this is a game that we are supposed to play. Not wanting to feel guilty because all of our friends were playing, we bought the stupid thing. They said that playing it would make you feel better about yourself; it would get you out of work and school; it would keep you out of trouble and make you feel like you were better than everyone else. I could have left mine sitting in the corner of my room, gathering dust like most of my other games. It could have remained buried underneath my Pictionary and Monopoly (The Anniversary Edition) and no one would have ever known that it was there. Or, I could have kept it hidden under my *Learn Mandarin Chinese in a Day* audio tapes and my *Memorize Your Way to Success in the Food Industry* DVD series. I was not that smart; I kept it out in the open where I was constantly reminded that it was there. I'd use it every chance I got.

Even though the game is ancient, it is not antiquated. The Blame Game is able to adapt to all new situations, across all cultures. You never need to purchase more parts, gadgets, upgrades (sorry Bill Gates), or accessories for the Game. That's the good news. The bad news: the game is usually purchased on credit. There are no obvious upfront costs, which is one reason that the game is owned by so many people. There are some class action law suits pending at the time of this writing against the manufacturer of the Blame Game for falsely advertising that the game is "free of any costs." However, no one admits to inventing the game.

Who can play?

Two cavemen walk into a bar and start buying drinks for everyone. The bartender asks, "What's the special occasion?" One cavemen answers, "We just finished a jigsaw puzzle and it only took three months to complete." The bartender says, "Three months? That seems like a long time for the two of you to finish a jigsaw puzzle." The caveman responds, "Oh ya? The box says three to five years!" Well, the Blame Game has no age limits. Everyone can and does play. Once purchased, this is a game that you can play until the moment you die.

Many do not realize that blaming was actually the first Game with active participants in every village, town, and city, in every county and country and on every continent. It is played equally by men and women, old and young, alike. Rosetta Stone, the popular language software program is available in thirty languages. The Monopoly game is licensed in 103 countries and is printed in thirty-seven languages including Icelandic and Croatian. This would be quite impressive yet these accomplishments pale in comparison to what blaming has achieved. The Blame Game is actively played by all inhabitants of every one of the 200 countries of the world. There are 6,912 known languages in the world. Blaming is played in every one of them! Blaming is also played in over 2,200 written languages! Most foreign editions of the game adopt their own culturally-sensitive and politically-correct accusational systems.

Some examples of blaming around the world:

- Blame in Danish is *skyld, beskylde, bebrejde, ansvar*
- Blame in Swedish is *klandra, skuld*
- Blame in Dutch is *beschuldigen, Blaam, de schuld geven aan, schuld, verantwoordelijk stellen, aanrekenen*
- Blame in German is blamieren, schuld, beschuldigen, die schuld geben
- Blame in Latin is *accuso, culpa, crimen*
- Blame in French is *accuser, blâme, blamer, faute, condemner, reproche*
- Blame in Norwegian is *klandre.*
- Blame in Canada is *blame, eh*
- Blame in Middle English was *blamen*
- Blame in Greek is ψέγω, μέμφομαι, κατακρίνω, καταφέρομαι εναντίον, κατηγορώ, ρίχνω την ευθύνη, υπαιτιότητα, ευθύνη, φταίξιμο
- Blame in Arabic is توبيخ, لوم (الاسم) وبخ, عاتب, لام (فعل)
- Blame in Hebrew is גינוי, אשמה, על אשמה הטיל, האשים
- Blame in Russian is *винить, порицать, осуждать, вина, порицание, осуждение*
- Blame in Croatian is *koriti, kriviti, krivnja, optužiti*

- Blame in Czech is *svádět, obviňování, obvinit, hana, svalovat vinu, obviňovat, dávat vinu, vina*
- Blame in Hungarian is *felelôsség, szemrehányás, vád*
- Blame in Turkish is *ayıplama kabahat, kusur azar, mesuliyet, azarlarnak, suçlamak, sorumlu tutmak*
- Blame in Hindi is दोष, दोष~लगाना, अपराधी~ठहराना
- Blame in Portuguese is *culpar, culpa, acusar*
- Blame in Italian is *accusare, accusa, rimproverare, olerne a, colpa, dare la colpa a, critica*
- Blame in Spanish is culpa, *reprender, reprimenda, reprension*
- Blame in Simple Chinese is 责备, 归咎于, 指责, 责任
- Blame in Traditional Chinese is 責備, 歸咎於, 責備, 指責, 責任
- Blame in Korean is 남을 비난하다, ~의 책임을 지우다, ~을 저주하다, 비난, 책임
- Blame in Japanese is ブラム, とがめる, 負わせる, 非難, とがめ, 責任

American Sign Language has also adopted the Game. To show "blame," take your right fist held vertically with your thumb pointed upward, your left hand flat out in front of you with your palm upward. Now sweep your right hand forward across your left palm, three times toward the person you are blaming. To sign "accuse," position your hands the same way and slightly bounce your right hand off the left, outward toward the accused. With a little practice, you'll be blaming and accusing in American Sign Language in no time at all.

There are no cultural borders with the Game. The Game appeals to those of all races, creeds, and colors. It is played by those from all sexual orientations, all religions and all ethnic groups. One of the most fascinating aspects about the Game is that participants most often enjoy playing it against people with whom they have little in common. It is quite frequent that blamers play the Game with complete strangers just as often as they do with close acquaintances. One would surmise that this would bring participants together in a bonding sort of group-hugging way. But sadly, the players frequently observe that the opposite is true. It is difficult to make friends playing the Blame Game. If you are team-blaming or group-blaming, those on your team or in your group will often develop a sense of camaraderie and loyalty during a round of blaming. However, these feelings of contentment do not last long. They dissipate rapidly and turn into feelings of distrust and concern about both the group and the LB (Lead Blamer). If the LB has true blaming expertise, he is quickly able to pronounce blame on anyone else in the group, which puts even their closest friends at risk.

What are the rules of The Game?

The list of rules is short. Many would consider the game quite intuitive and have long since thrown away their instruction manual. Truth be told, the original instruction manual only states, "Blame everyone. Blame often. Blame when in doubt and blame when you have no doubt. Blame those you love and blame strangers as well. Do not blame with discrimination; be an equal opportunity blamer." Although all of us start this game at a very young age, we do get better with practice. Like in most sports, playing more often typically allows you to acquire more advanced blaming techniques. The Game becomes very natural to most of us and becomes almost second nature.

Blaming is legally allowed in both verbal and written formats, with long traditions for both. The first governing body of blaming began as a rather undisciplined group of unemployed complainers in the early 1700s in Washington, D.C. They called themselves the "Big Group of Blame Unto Thee and Those Society (Big BUTTS). With a growing group of followers and an expanding base of unemployed persons across the country, the name of the organization changed in the late 1700s to the National Office of Blamers (NOBs). As blaming groups and societies sprang up around the world in the mid-1800s, international pressure grew to create some type of global governing body, the NOBs expanded their association into what is now the International Blaming Federation (IBF). It wasn't long after the official formation of the IBF before there was internal strife. The IBF was not doing well financially and there were many accusations of graft and dirty politics.

There were those who would stand up in front of the entire society's membership and blame the senior leadership for the woes of the Federation while others started a written "Campaign of Blame" to achieve the same end. These two groups quickly became rival factions and started blaming each other for their lack of progress. The Verbal Blamers gave lectures about the problems in both the IBF and in the rest of the world, while the Written Blamers started and continue to publish the journal, *Blamers Quarterly* (BQ). In the mid-1920s the two groups were able to come to some agreements and decided to create sub-associations within the IBF: the Written Blame Association (WBA) and the Verbal Blame Association (VBA).

There were those who predicted that blaming would not be able to make a smooth transition to the computer age. However, with the advent of personal computers, the frequency of blaming has skyrocketed. For anyone interested in perusing the tens of thousands of blaming references on the Internet, search the term "blame" in combination with any famous proper name, country name, name of a group, or even inanimate objects or events. The Internet truly excels in its role as a Blame Documentation Device (BDD).

When will The Game end?

What is the goal of the Game? The one who delivers the most blames wins. There are several blaming options available. You can play for cumulative points throughout your lifetime or you can play to see who the first person is to deliver one hundred blames. Experts can complete this within nineteen minutes; the world record for one hundred unique blames was fourteen minutes and twenty seconds. The record was set by Annie Wonbutt-Me in 1978; a record that is still well-respected within the blaming community. One may also choose to play the Blame Game on a week-by-week basis. How many blames delivered in one week? Some have been known to play The Game by trying to deliver either the most unique blame or the most unexpected blame or the most unpredictable blame, or the most convincing blame. You can also try to come up with the best blame for each of the categories described in the "How To Blame" chapter. Take turns blaming and then after each round, the players decide whose blame was the best in a given category. Limit play to blaming people or blaming things or blaming groups, etc. There are endless hours of play once you are familiar with blaming. When you decide that you've had enough ("Blamed out"), the Game is over. Accuse others so that you can feel better about yourself. That pretty much sums up the Game's objective.

As in most cases of addiction, most people don't realize that they have a need to continue blaming. As the Game is rather simple to play, they have convinced themselves and others that they enjoy the Game and actually benefit from playing it. This makes voluntarily ending the Game extremely difficult—especially in view of the fact that there have been no documented cases of anyone having accomplished this. I do not claim to be able to show you how to quit, since I have not been successful at doing this myself. However, I will show you ways that you can start reducing your playing time and feel much better about yourself and others once you are able do this.

2. Some Blaming Formats

"Democracy is the process by which people choose the man who'll get the blame."

Bertrand Russell

There exist several forms of Blaming of which you should be aware. We'll focus on three common varieties: *Group Blaming, Televised Blaming,* and *Legal Blaming.* Group Blaming has been undeniably responsible for changing the face of the earth. It has changed and destroyed countless cultures and peoples since the dawn of time. Televised Blaming has become much more popular as television, broadcast to worldwide audiences, is internationally appealing. Legal Blaming is a book by itself. Anyone lucky enough to have been involved in the legal system will readily realize that lawsuits are simply "Legal Blames."

Group blaming

Group Blaming has the greatest potential for changing the state of the world. Group Blaming is and was the cause of every war since the beginning of time. All disputes between countries and continents; all civil wars; all world wars, were the result of Group Blaming. Sure, they might have started out as Innocent Blames, but look where they got us. Whether you are talking about African Americans, Jews, Protestants, Tutsis, Women, Homosexuals, etc., there has never been a documented case in history where Group Blaming was actually beneficial to the Group that was doing the blaming and it certainly hasn't been the cause of a great deal of celebration among the groups being blamed. Group Blame causes all wars, rapes, pillaging, racism, persecution, and riots. Blaming groups of people for acting in certain ways or for having certain beliefs that are inconsistent with our own often leads to violence.

Cavemen are responsible for some of your problems; I'm not making this up. Patricia Neighmond, writing for National Public Radio, asks, "Why do we seem to relish salty, sweet, high-fat and fried foods? Scientists studying the biology of hunger say our cravings for the unhealthy may have a lot to do with evolution." In the article, *Jonesing for Fries? Blame the Cave Men,* Gary Beauchamp, director of Monell Chemical Senses Center, says our human ancestors were largely herbivores, making the consumption of adequate calories a greater challenge. While we are no longer a society of herbivores, we have maintained the genetic predisposition for caloric craving. Attributing our poor diets, fatty foods, lack of fruits and vegetables, and overconsumption to poor self-control and perhaps a lack of education would suggest that the control and responsibility for our weight lies within each of us. However, with this new theory regarding hunger biology, we can gain as much weight as we want, eat poorly, show that we are not strong enough to resist urges in our diet, and still feel great because we are able to blame our lack of control and obesity on prehistoric cavemen. What a deal!

Slavery is at fault. Yes, slavery would not have occurred if there was no blame. Some blame the origins of the evils of slavery on Africans who were involved in bringing slaves to the African coast for sale to slave traders. Some blame racism. Most in the North blamed the South, and many Southerners blamed the North for slavery. Those folks north of the Mason-Dixon Line could be blamed because the New England-based ships did business with the African chieftains selling their conquered enemies into slavery and thus facilitating the slave trade. While many in the North argued that slaves were not property, Northern corporate America profited by insuring slaves as property. There was no IRS or personal income tax prior to the Civil War; so much of the United States government revenue was derived from tariffs placed on the export of cotton picked by slaves in the South. The North controlled the congressional votes that determined how revenue was spent and thus much of this revenue was spent in the North to help build its infrastructure. This disproportionate spending was one reason for the South's interest in secession from the Union. Most in the United States blamed slavery on the cost of running the country.

Christians were persecuted by the Romans. The security of the state was attributed to worshipping and leaving sacrifices for the Roman gods, including Mars, Jupiter, and Poseidon. Christians, finding this practice abhorrent, incurred Roman blame, especially during troubled times, and were thrown to the lions. One of the most famous blames was in A.D. 64 when there was a great fire that destroyed much of Rome. Many believed that the fire was actually started by the Emperor, Nero, who did not like Rome. Nero started a rumor that the Christians were actually to blame for starting the fire and this gave him another good reason for having them put to death.

Jews were erroneously blamed for killing Jesus. Mel Gibson helped resurrect this blame, reviving and reinvigorating negative feelings toward Jews, especially in Europe. Jews have also been associated with managing successful businesses in countries that were otherwise not well-off financially. Jews often acted as royal advisors and bankers. In these roles, they were felt to wield unrestricted power, and jealousy became rampant. Such was the case in England, Spain, Portugal, and several other European countries. The year 1492 was not only the year that Columbus set sail for the New World, but it was also the year that Jews were forcibly expelled from Spain by virtue of the Alhambra Decree (which was not revoked until 1968). Jews were given three months to convert, leave Spain, or face death. Thus several of these Jews (and former Jews forced to convert), ac- companied Columbus and we can blame them, in part, for the discovery and eventual settlements in the United States.

Israel has been blamed for most of the violence in the middle East. While there is some overlap with the above paragraph on Jews, these are indeed two separate blaming targets. There is some component of anti-Semitism in anti-Israel blaming, yet there is also some specific anti-Zionist sentiment. Israel is blamed as "the agent" which pushes the Palestinians and Islamic world to commit violent actions. This type of thinking is actually racist against the Palestinians also, insinuating that they have no independent moral compass and are only capable of responding in a vicious manner. In November 2014, two Palestinian terrorists savagely killed worshippers praying in a Jerusalem synagogue. Somehow international reports were able to implicate Israel. CNN reported, "4 Israelis, 2 Palestinians dead in Jerusalem", without noting that the two Palestinians were the terrorists. During the Gaza war while thousands of rockets were launched with the goal of killing Israeli civilians, the Obama administration blamed Israel for the deaths of Palestinians who were used as human shields by Hamas. It is "in vogue" to blame Israel for the world woes.

In 2013 the UN General Assembly adopted a total of 21 resolutions singling out Israel for criticism…and 4 resolutions on the rest of the world combined (Syria, Iran, North Korea, and Myanmar). There were no resolutions on gross abuses committed by China, Saudi Arabia, Cuba, Egypt, Iraq, Qatar, Russia, Pakistan, Russia, Sri Lanka, Sudan, Lebanon, or Zimbabwe. Israel is the target of overt bias and blame and at least 77 UN resolutions. There is one UN resolution against the Palestinians. Supermarkets have removed products from Israel, there are multiple Israeli boycotts, and anti-Israel protests have propagated throughout Europe and the United States. The fact that the majority of Israelis (including those in the government) want peace with their Arab neighbors and is a democratic ally is ignored. The fact that Palestinians in Gaza call for the uncompromising destruction of Israel, incite violence, and celebrate when Israeli civilians are murdered is also ignored.

Homosexuals have been blamed for the current crisis of child sexual abuse by priests. Homosexuals have also been blamed for AIDS, pedophilia, and gender variance. Headline in *USA TODAY* in 2002: is homosexuality to blame for church scandal?

Homosexuality is not the same as pedophilia. Homosexuals are no more likely than heterosexuals to molest children. Obviously, homosexuals did not cause the AIDS virus, nor are they responsible for gender preferences.

Women are blamed for many things in our society. In an online newsletter, called TheAge.com.au, Karen Murphy wrote an article titled, "Blame Women for the Death of Feminism." Women have been blamed for much sexual violence that occurs. The BBC has reported that a third of people surveyed believe that a woman who flirts is at least partially to blame for being raped. In 2006, a senior Australian Muslim cleric similarly blamed women for being raped. He stated that if women stayed in their rooms, in their homes, wearing headscarves, this would solve the problem.

Women also blame women for the state of girls' self-image today and for eating disorders. As an example of how successful the campaign has been to blame the female gender, you can even log on to the BlameWomen.com website.

Women have been accused of being responsible for everything that goes wrong with children, from having them to raising them. And working mothers make their kids fat. According to economists Patricia Anderson, Kristin Butcher and Phillip Levine, even ten hours a week of maternal employment ups a child's chances of becoming overweight. This accusation, of course relieves fathers of any accountability in the raising of their children.

Women have also been blamed for the situation in Iraq, illegal immigration, bad office morale, bad pets, and homosexuality. In 2006, the Tennessee Guerilla Women Blog asked, "Can We Blame Women for Global Warming?"

Men don't get a free pass. Recently men were blamed for the majority of human genetic mutations, according to a publication in the scientific journal *Nature*. Researchers of the Human Genome Project discovered that the Y chromosome, found only in men, passes on genetic mutations twice as often as the X chromosome. Women have two X chromosomes while men have one X and one Y. Men create billions of sperm in their lifetime, while women produce only a few hundred eggs and the rate of mutation appears to be higher in sperm production than in egg production. So while men can be blamed for most genetic mutations, we should realize that some of these mutations involve resistance to infections and certain diseases, improved senses, maybe even higher intelligence. Those are good things for which to be blamed.

Let's take a look at something that men know virtually nothing about: premenstrual syndrome (or PMS). Around 75-80 percent of women suffer from PMS. For decades, hormonal changes were to blame for the symptoms of tiredness, irritability, mood swings, and cravings for sugary foods. Now, Fiona Macrae of the Daily Mail reported "Men to Blame for PMS." How can this happen? Psychology Professor Jane Ussher from the University of Western Sydney claims that, "Men certainly play a significant role in PMS and can play a very significant role in women's depression and anger at that time of the cycle." Since hormones are continually changing, is it fair to say that men may always be held accountable for a women's mood and energy level? Is it also fair to say then that a man is able to blame a woman for driving him to drink?

Jenna Brooke, a personal and professional coach, has written an online article titled "Let's Blame Men." Ann Zak, in the Department of Psychology at the College of Saint Rose, published a study looking at men and women's perception of relationships. Given a hypothetical situation with equal responsibility, females more often blamed males for couples experiencing conflict (we should note that men more often blamed females for the same situations).

Americans are not the victims—they are to blame! There have now been multiple attacks on the American infrastructure, the World Trade Center, the Twin Towers, and the continued assault on American and European interests by Islamic Extremists. While not representative of most Muslims, there are several among the radical factions who blame Western culture itself for these acts of violence. For example, the *New York Times* (http://www.nytimes.com/2005/11/14/opinion/14iht-edkhouri.html) in 2005 asked, "Amman Attack: Is America to Blame?" This article suggested that America's support of Israel and anti-terrorist policies that have spread to certain Arab nations may be to blame for any attack by an extremist group. As infidels, America and other non-Islamic nations have brought violence upon themselves.

Northern Ireland is the center of the Blaming World. When we think of Group Blame it is hard to avoid the conflict in the north of Ireland. An article published in *American Foreign Policy Interests*, in June 2005 was titled "The Blame Game in Northern Ireland." Colin Irwin in the March/June 2003 issue of the *Global Review of Ethnopolitics* writes, "One of the most popular cross community activities in Northern Ireland is playing the 'Blame Game.'"

Eighty-four percent of Sinn Féin (Irish Republican Party Nationalists seeking to end British rule in Northern Ireland— predominantly Catholic) supporters blame Unionists (who want a Union with Great Britain — predominantly Protestant) and 82 percent of Democratic Unionist Party supporters blame Republicans. Everyone was quite even-handed when it came to blaming the two governments at 58 percent for Protestants, 56 percent for Catholics, 55 percent for Democratic Unionist Party supporters, 60 percent for the Ulster Unionist Party, 51 percent for the Social Democratic and Labour Party, and 60 percent for Sinn Féin. It's easy to see how slowly moving this peace process remains when there is so much blame being distributed. It is hard to move beyond the blame to more productive stages.

World War I provided a plethora of blames. On June 28, 1914, Gavrilo Princip, a Bosnian-Serb student and member of Young Bosnia (a group whose aims included the unification of the South Slavs and independence from Austria-Hungary), shot and killed Archduke Franz Ferdinand who was heir to the Austro-Hungarian throne. The assassination set into motion a series of Group Blames that eventually escalated into full-scale war. Major European powers were at war within weeks because of International Group Blame agreements. The Austro-Hungarian government blamed the assassination of the Archduke as a pretext to deal with what they termed the Serbian question. President Woodrow Wilson of the United States blamed the war on militarism. Vladimir Lenin of the Soviet Union blamed the war on imperialism. Cordell Hull, American Secretary of State under Franklin Roosevelt, believed that trade barriers were to blame for World War I.

The result: over forty million casualties, including approximately twenty million military and civilian deaths. The Entente Powers, led by France, Russia, the British Empire, and later Italy and the United States, defeated the Central Powers, led by the Austro-Hungarian, German, and Ottoman Empires.

So who was really at fault? Blame was at fault; I term this "autoblame." It should be noted that according to *BQ* magazine, autoblame is what you do when your car won't start or we have to bail out GM with another twenty billion dollars ... don't get me started. I would contend that placing the blame squarely on blame is acceptable in this case and every other case where war and vast destruction is incurred.

World War II was the blame to end all blames. German dictator Adolf Hitler's Nazi Party sought to blame Germany's "humiliating" status on the harshness of the post-war settlement, the weakness of the democratic government, and on the Jews. It was this blame that led to humanity's deadliest and most destructive war. The number of estimated lives taken were 72 million people including: 19 million Russians, 6 million Jews, 2.5 million Poles, 1.3 million Yugoslovakians, 500,000 Gypsies and 400,000 Greeks.

Vietnam is still being blamed for dividing two countries. The U.S. involvement in the Korean War and the Vietnam War were blamed on communism. General Dwight D. Eisenhower, as the new President in 1953, cites a "Domino Theory" in which a Communist victory in Vietnam would result in surrounding countries falling one after another. The North Vietnamese blamed the United States for attacks on two North Vietnamese islands, Hon Me and Hon Nieu, during Operation 34A, which was a secret plan of naval attacks by the United States. The North Vietnamese then attacked an American destroyer, the USS *Maddox* in August 1964; less than a week later, a second torpedo attack in the same gulf (Gulf of Tonkin) against the United States was reported. CBS newsman Walter Cronkite was later quoted as saying that the sonar data from the second attack could have been produced by an incontinent whale. The situation was construed as an attack on U.S. forces and the North Vietnamese were blamed. The U.S. Congress then passed the Gulf of Tonkin Resolution, granting President Lyndon B. Johnson sweeping war powers and allowing U.S. involvement in Vietnam to escalate.

Darfur, an area in western Sudan, has seen the genocide of over 450,000 lives at the hands of the government and government-sponsored militia. About 2.3 million Darfuris have fled their homes. While the "conflict" is blamed on ethnic and tribal differences, all Darfuris are and black. The distinction lies in whether they are

"African" or "Arab." With lower rainfall and desertification, Arab nomads would travel with their livestock into non-Arab areas for water. The Arabs along with the Sudanese government have blamed the decades of drought, lack of water, and overpopulation as an excuse to wipe out an entire group of people.

The Iraq invasion in 2003 was blamed on the Iraqi leader, Saddam Hussein, for possessing and actively developing weapons of mass destruction, which has now turned out to be of questionable validity. Our continued presence there is blamed by right-wing conservatives in the United States on the Iraqi insurgency and civil war between Sunni and Shia Iraqis. In contrast, liberals in the United States blame former President George W. Bush for the war. President Obama blamed George Bush for our continued presence in Iraq, but now that Obama is president, he finds it harder to bring the troops home than he previously thought. In the State of the Union address in 2010, President Obama stopped blaming former President Bush for our presence in Iraq and instead he took credit for the United States successes in that country – only pass the blame; not the acclaim.

Afghanistan is a hot issue plaguing the Obama White House Blaming George Bush for the United States involvement in Afghanistan has worked very well for many months. However, during this important time of focusing on blaming, we still haven't reached a decision about the plans for U.S. troops. President Obama and Vice President Biden still blame former president George Bush for not leaving them specific war plans. Republicans blame the Obama administration for not being accountable. It will be interesting as to when a responsibility shift will occur; when it becomes Obama's plan and war.

Blaming in the Media

The most popular venues for viewing blaming on television are talk shows, reality shows, and presidential debates.

Talk Shows. If talk show hosts are not blaming someone for something in a monologue, then the guest must take on the role of shifting responsibility and blaming somebody for some event or wrongdoing in their lives or in the world as we know it. Let's look at a few real-life examples.

Wildfires. Actual news headline from Journalism.org, October 2007: talk hosts play the blame game with California fires. There were rampaging wildfires in California in 2007. Some fires were naturally occurring and some were started by arsonists. When it came time for the discussion about the fires, liberal talk show radio host Randi Rhodes took the opportunity to blame former President George Bush and referred to statements that he had made immediately following Hurricane Katrina in which he praised the Federal Emergency Management Agency (FEMA) director for his response to the hurricane. Other liberal talk show hosts and guests blamed the federal government for lack of sufficient firefighting funds. On the other side of the political fence, conservative radio hosts Rush Limbaugh, Sean Hannity, and Bill O'Reilly linked the fires that destroyed about two thousand homes to elements of the environmental movement. They accused those who connected the fires to global warming of "a blatant attempt to politicize" the disaster. Limbaugh laid blame on the "whacko environmentalists who will not let anybody go in and clear out the dead wood." Hannity attributed blame to the environmentalists not allowing "thinning of forests to prevent wildfires."

Mugging. News headline from PajamasMedia: liberal talk show host Randi Rhodes is mugged, liberals immediately blame conservatives, from October 16, 2007. The report explained that liberal talk radio host Randi Rhodes was assaulted in New York while walking her dog. According to the report she was beaten to the point of losing teeth in the attack. The liberal *Air America* show immediately blamed Conservatives and the "right wing hate machine..." who wanted to silence her by viciously attacking her. The follow-up as reported by the *New York Daily News*—there was no mugging. She fell down while she was walking her dog. Sorry, who do we blame now? Maybe we can blame the cement worker who laid the sidewalk or the city contractor who bid the job for the sidewalk to be installed, or... could we blame the puppy?

Teddy Bear. Headline from NewsBusters.org by Justin McCarthy: 'view' co-hosts blame woman persecuted by Sudan. In November, 2007, a British woman was teaching at a school in

Sudan. One child in the class wanted to name a teddy bear Muhammad and the woman agreed, unaware that this violated Islamic law. She was arrested while the Sudanese government decided between stoning and lashing. The hosts of the talk show *The View* did not direct anger at the Sudanese government, but blamed the woman for not adapting to the culture.

Jenny Jones. The talk show host Jenny Jones brought Mr. Schmitz on her show to be surprised by a "secret crush." The crush turned out to be a man who, three days later was shot and killed by Mr. Schmitz. This man's family successfully blamed and sued the talk show for $25 million. They contended that the show should have realized that Mr. Schmitz had a history of mental illness and that the humiliation would have been too much for him to bear.

Writers' Strike. In 2007, there was a television writers' strike that all but crippled popular talk shows. An article in *Variety* magazine by Brian Lowry blamed the strike on the "Rush Limbaugh era of talk radio …" He asserts that Conservative talk shows fuel the fire of debate and cause a "poisonous environment" where in the past there was no "us" versus "them" philosophy. Of course the writers blame the people who previously supplied their paychecks. The owners blame the writers for wanting in excess, the hosts blame …

Benghazi. September 11, 2012, the American Embassy in Benghazi attacked killing Ambassador Christopher Stephens and three other Americans. How did this horrible event happen? In the fifteen days following the attacks, President Obama, Secretary of State Hillary Clinton, UN Ambassador Susan Rice, and Press Secretary Jay Carney publicly blamed an anti-Muslim YouTube video no less than seven times. It was later revealed that indeed the administration already knew that the video was not involved. The massacre was lead by terrorists and not a spontaneous angry mob. A bipartisan report from the Senate Intelligence committee blamed the State Department for failing to increase security to protect the personnel in light of increased security threats. The Republicans claim that the ultimate blame lay with Secretary of State, Hillary Clinton and the democrats are to be blamed for a cover-up of their inadequacies. The democrats retort that the Republicans are to blame for turning this tragedy into a politically-motivated witch-hunt.

Virginia Tech Massacre. Cho Seung Hui shot and killed thirty-three people at Virginia Technical College in 2007. There were many stories about this young man's history, how he slipped by authorities and how many warning signs existed. *The Daily Show* with Jon Stewart asked the question, "Who's to Blame for VA Tech Massacre?" Lax gun control laws? Strict gun control laws? Liberals? Rosie O'Donnell? Television? Hollywood? Video Games? Society? YouTube? He plays a round of the Blame Game with several possible blamees. Karate and TV star Chuck Norris, on the WorldNetDaily website (www.wnd.com), blames the "Secular Progressive Agenda." A caller on the Rush Limbaugh show also blamed the massacre on violent video games. Thankfully, Mr. Limbaugh recognized that while Cho may have played these games, "not every video gamer goes out and murders thirty-three people on the college campus." People are responsible for their own actions. A blog posting by "Chris" on www.cynical-c.com is dedicated to the Blame Game for the Virginia Tech massacre:

It's the fault of violent video games.
It's the fault of movies.
It's that no other students were armed.
It's the cowardly students who didn't rush the shooter.
It's the first victim's fault.
It's secularism's fault.
It's the Muslims' and/or foreigners' fault.
It's the Atheists' fault.
It's the fault of the colleges and how they coddle their students.
It's society's fault.
It's the Second Amendment's
fault. It's the bureaucracy's fault.
It's the fault of Roanoke Firearms, where he bought the gun.
It's the authorities' fault.
It's the Liberals' fault.
It's pedophilia, homosexual couplings, and adulterous behavior's fault.
It's capitalism's fault.
It's the fault of psychiatric drugs.

It's the Devil's fault.
It's South Korea's fault.
It's the hippies' fault. (Nobody's blaming the Yippies yet.)
It's the media and culture's fault.
It's the murderer's fault. It's the legal system's fault.
It's the fault of the Virginia Tech officials.
It's the fault of the Chinese.
It's the fault of this blogger who happens to be Asian, likes guns, and who recently broke up with his girlfriend.
It's Simon Cowell's fault.
It's Bill Gates' fault.
It's the fault of trauma-induced mind control by a military industrial complex.
It's the killer's parents' and/or gun makers' fault.
It's the fault that colleges have co-ed dorms and/or students who major in English.
It's a lack of funding for mental health services' fault.
It's the GOP's fault.
It's the Democrats' fault.
It's NBC's fault.
It's Autism's fault.
It's al Jazeera or Palestinian TV's fault.
It's the fault of pro-choice doctors.
It's Collective Soul's fault.
It's the fault of professors who survived the Holocaust and are not armed to the teeth.
It's Markos from the Daily Kos' fault.
It's the bullies' fault.
It's the Nanjing Anti-African riots' fault and/or the fault of those in interracial relationships.
It's the fault of our culture's all-consuming desire for celebrity. It's fault of the Europeanization or nannyization of American behavior.
It's Charlton Heston's fault.
It's the fault of immigration and/or Asians.
It's evil's fault.
It's W's fault.
It's the fault of vaccines.
It's the fault that schools teach that the theory of evolution is fact.

It's the fault of the CIA for training the killer as a mind-controlled assassin.
It's the fault of stage weapons used in school plays.
It's the fault of the classes where Cho was taught to hate.
It's the school's architecture's fault.
It's the fault of those who voted for Ralph Nader.
It's the fault of Bill Clinton, Internet pornography, free speech, condoms, abortions, and lack of prayer and bibles in schools.
It's that Cho didn't hook up enough.
It's the fault of the Jews.
It's the ACLU's fault.
It's the fault of media glorification.
It's the fault of Americans.
It's the fault of America's youth mentality.
It's the fault of big business.
It's the fault of college admissions.
It's the fault of his roommates for being too politically correct.
It's the fault of the psychiatrist who let Cho get away.
It's the fault of progressive education.
It's the fault of white women.
It's the ideology of diversity's fault.
It's Cho's High School's fault.
It's Dateline's fault.

Oklahoma City Federal Building. In 1995 the Oklahoma City Federal Building was bombed by U.S. anti-government fanatics. President Bill Clinton blamed the "purveyors of hatred and division," referring to extremist radio talk shows. He stated that such talk shows "spread hate" and leave the impression that "violence is acceptable." Many such shows focused on confrontations, emotional violence, and sexual messages with socially unacceptable behavior. Oprah Winfrey actually broke the trend, initially losing some viewers, yet later gaining popularity with some positive messages conveyed in her book club.

Twin Towers. Following the September 11, 2001, terrorist attacks on the Twin Towers, there were several precautionary statements made, including those by the Seattle Police, to tone down anti-Muslim rhetoric for fear of further attacks. Liberals blamed conservative talk radio and political policies, while televangelists Pat Robertson and Jerry Falwell blamed liberals, feminists, and abortion-rights advocates. Many talk show hosts briefly turned down their confrontational tone. There were those in the news who blamed Americans for their pro-Israel policies and there were those in the news who blamed a Jewish conspiracy.

Northern Ireland. As written above, Northern Ireland is a hotbed of blaming. In fact, *Farber's Travel Guide: Where to Blame in Ireland for Less Than $5 Per Day* has documented Northern Ireland to be one of the "best blaming locations in the world." The Blame Game Television Show in Northern Ireland is an actual talk show that began as a BBC broadcast. This show truly exemplifies what it means to actually make blame assignments. "This is done in an attempt to clear ourselves of any responsibility," states one of the show's writers. "We perhaps should have called it, *It's Not My Fault*, the irony being, if you don't like the show you can blame me."

The Credit Crisis. In 2008, the banks went bad; mortgage companies went bad; the stock market went bad. As par for the course, Democrats blamed Republicans for providing us with such a bad economy and increasing the national debt. Republicans blamed Democrats for setting up a system whereby mortgages were given to people that couldn't qualify for them. Both Democrats and Re- publicans agreed to write blank checks totaling more than $800 billion to bail out financial institutions and mortgage companies.

This was soon followed in February of 2009 with the biggest spending bill known to man, with close to another $800 billion to "jump start" the economy. Again, Democrats blamed Republicans for getting us in this mess and Republicans blamed Democrats for getting us in this mess. The Democrats passed the spending bills without Republican support. So, if the stimulus/pork project succeeds, Democrats can take credit for the success and, with great pride, blame conservatives for wanting to try "more of the same old methods." If the stimulus/pork package doesn't work, Repubicans can claim victory and blame liberals as America goes further into recession. David Merkel, CFA, wrote a posting on Alephblog.com called, you guessed it—"The Blame Game." Mr.

The Blame Game

Merkel describes who's to blame for the crisis. Here's his list (plus a few additions from his blog list).

1) The Federal Reserve, especially Alan Greenspan.
2) Congress and the presidency—for encouraging undue leverage:
   a) Fannie, Freddie, the FHLB (Federal Home Loan Banks): Everyone has gotta live in a single family home.
   b) The SEC (Security and Exchange Commission): Waived leverage restrictions on the investment banks in 2004, leading to a boom, and a bust.
   c) Particularly the Democrats in Congress defended the government sponsored enterprises.
   d) We offered a tax deduction on mortgage interest, and a limited exemption on capital gains from selling a home. There is no good reason for these measures.
   e) And, the Republicans in Congress who favored deregulation in areas for which it was foolish to deregulate.
   f) The Bush Jr. Administration—did not enforce regulations over financial institutions the way that the law would demand on a fair reading.
   g) Their unfunded programs with promises to the future.
3) Lenders steered borrowers to bad loans.
4) Borrowers were lazy and greedy.
5) Appraisers were slaves of the lenders who wanted to originate and sell.
6) Those that originated mortgage-backed security did not check the creditworthiness adequately.
7) Servicers did not demand a high price for their services.
8) Realtors steered people into buying more than they could rationally afford.
9) Mortgage insurers and financial guarantee insurers—they were able to offer guarantees significantly in excess of what they could pay.
10) Hedge funds, investment banks and their investors—they demanded returns that were higher than what was sustainable.
11) Regulators let themselves be compromised by those

following the profit motive.
12) America. We let ourselves become short-term as a culture... regardless of the cost.
13) Neomercantilists—they lent us money... This made our interest rates too low, encouraging overinvestment and overconsumption.
14) Average people who voted in Congress and demanded perpetual prosperity...
15) Auditors that did a cursory job auditing financial entities.
16) Rating agencies.
17) The Office of the Comptroller of the Currency.
18) The carry traders and flippers.
19) Academics who encouraged a naive view of diversification.
20) Pension and other funds that believed the academics.
21) Governmental entities that happily expanded government programs as the boom went on.
22) Those that twitted "doom-and-gloomers," and investors who only cared if markets went up.
23) Me [Mr. Merkel], and others who warned about the current crisis. Perhaps we weren't clear enough.

As in other lists of blamees, Mr. Merkel informs us that his list is not complete.

Talk shows push the envelope of what is exciting and outrageous. They compete to outdo each other with shocking behavior and *Blatant Blames*. From reality-based talk shows like Jerry Springer, where the Blame Game is played from the beginning until the end of each episode, we now enjoy reality-based television. Everyone on a talk show has an agenda, whether it is political or simply a matter of achieving recognition and fortune. Capturing their fifteen minutes of fame or prolonging their notoriety is believed to be best achieved through blaming.

Reality Shows: Are you a bachelor, bachelorette, bisexual performer, survivor, or college student? Do you aspire to have a career in singing, dancing, porn, photography, cooking, acting, mixed martial arts, or boxing? Are you a little person, big person, need to gain weight, lose weight, or just get stronger, faster, or smarter? Need a date, or does your mom or dad need a date? Are you not getting along with your spouse, family or friends and need someone to blame in front of a national audience? If so, there exists a reality show just for you. If you don't fit into any one of these profiles and your urge and need to blame nationally in a televised setting is imperative, be patient, I'm sure a reality show for you will soon be in production. One might better term these shows as "Blame-A-thons." Watching people whom we believe are acting spontaneously and, for the most part are unhappy with their lives and constantly blaming others for their plight, is addictive. Producers produce what we consume. So ... don't blame them!

Presidential Debates: Hubert H. Humphrey (38th U.S. vice president) stated, "We believe that to err is human. To blame it on someone else is politics." We watch with interest the presidential debates in which each candidate either directly or indirectly blames some other candidate or the current president for the current state of disaster and disrepair. When you watch a televised presidential debate, imagine that you're viewing a blaming contest. Try to see who has the most creative blames. Who provides the most mildly-appearing, yet dramatically-insinuating accusations? This will make the debates even more entertaining for you. Obviously, throughout the campaign, the Democrats blame the Republicans and the Republicans blame the Democrats. However, in the early stages of presidential elections, the candidates blame members from their own party as they vie for a spot in the primary election. The presidential debates remain one of the more important initiations into the democratic process whereby, as Mr. Russell suggested, we can begin to establish who will take on the elected role of Chief Blamee.

Legal Blaming

Have you ever been involved in the legal system in any way? Have you spoken with a lawyer, watched some courtroom session on television, or just heard about some large legal settlement on the radio? If so, you have witnessed Blaming perfection. The legal system has taken blaming to the next level of play. When someone files a lawsuit, it is to claim that someone else was at fault for whatever it is that occurred. I don't blame the lawyers for this. Everyone enjoys playing the Blame Game and the legal profession is simply capitalizing on our love of the game.

The book entitled, *Legal Blame: How Jurors Think and Talk About Accidents* by Neal Feigenson, helps explain how the legal system and jurors determine and assign fault. Legally and realistically, every action sets in motion a chain of events. Blame can be placed if the results of one's actions are foreseeable or if they can be causally-related in a reasonable chain of events. In fact, the legal term, "negligence," which on the surface sounds somewhat innocent and without intention or willfulness, means conduct that is blamable because it is what is expected of a "reasonable person" in protecting individuals against foreseeably risky, harmful acts. Negligent behavior towards others gives them the right to be compensated for harm that they incur to their body, property, mental well-being, financial status, or relationships.

In 1984, there was a case in Australia of *Jaensch v. Coffey*. The court upheld that Mrs. Coffey incurred a nervous shock injury from the aftermath of a motor vehicle accident in which she was not even at the scene. Mr. Jaensch was involved in an accident with Mrs. Coffey's husband, who was a policeman. Upon hearing the news and after waiting at the hospital throughout several of her husband's surgeries, Mrs. Coffey suffered severe anxiety and depression. Her mental state was said to subsequently lead to gynecological problems, which then resulted in a hysterectomy. The legal Blame Game often involves a chain of events. In this case the court found that indeed there was a Blame Chain or legal Chain of Blame (CoB) and that the outcome should have been foreseeable by Mr. Jaensch.

In reference to the September 11, 2001, attacks on the Twin Towers, an organization known as Magniloquence Against War claims, "We do not blame America first. In fact, we never blame America at all." Here's their CoB:

1. We blame the hijackers.
2. We blame the organization that planned the attacks and prepared the hijackers for their mission.
3. We blame the supporters of that organization.
4. We blame the social and economic conditions that contribute

to support for that organization.
5. We blame the aspects of American foreign policy that contribute to those conditions.
6. We blame the American Central Intelligence Agency, who provided the leaders of the organization behind the attacks with high-tech weaponry and training in military strategy and sabotage.
7. We blame American politicians, including Ronald Reagan and George Herbert Walker Bush, who approved the gifts of military training and weapons to the organization behind the attacks and developed the foreign policies that contribute to the social and economic conditions underlying support for that organization.
8. We blame the American citizens who voted for those politicians.

While this CoB is quite extensive, it leaves out many details including many radical groups and countries that have supported terror organizations either directly by supplying weapons and/or money or by turning a blind eye. Their blaming list included Presidents Reagan and Bush but neglected Bill Clinton who also had chances to do something about the growing al Qaeda threat during his tenure in office. In 1996, after being presented with evidence implicating bin Laden in embassy attacks and suggesting his involvement in weapons of mass destruction, Clinton ordered missile strikes upon training camps and added bin Laden to the list of terrorists whose assets are targeted for seizure by the United States. The United States appeared to play the role of the bully and drew criticism from the Muslim world. In 1998 and 1999, interviews with bin Laden ran in Time and Newsweek describing his hatred for the West and Israel. He called for all American males to be killed. There were no significant attempts by the Clinton administration to bring this group's activities to an end. While they may not have predicted the extent of the outcome, they should still be added to the list.

Social psychologists refer to a human web, where all humans are connected by a maximum of six degrees of separation. This concept was made famous by a screenplay of the same name as well as a popular game. In the game Six Degrees of Kevin Bacon, the challenge is to link any actor or actress to Kevin Bacon with no more than six connections. At *Magniloquence Against War* they have stated that in their chain of blame, "there are eight degrees of blame separating a particular bloc of American voters from the September 11 attacks." Conclusion: We are all to blame.

During the 2008 election campaign, President Barack Obama's pastor, Rev. Jeremiah Wright, the longtime leader of Trinity United Church of Christ drew great attention by saying that the United States brought on the Sept. 11, 2001, attacks with its own "terrorism." "We bombed Hiroshima, we bombed Nagasaki, and we nuked far more than the thousands in New York and the Pentagon, and we never batted an eye," Wright said on Sept. 16, 2001. "God damn America for treating our citizens as less than human. God damn America for as long as she acts like she is God and she is supreme," Wright said in a 2003 sermon. Blaming the victim of a terrorist attack is akin to blaming the victim of sexual abuse. Neither is fair blame! He continues to blame America for its capitalism, of which he hypocritically and enthusiastically enjoys.

A marvelous CoB, "The Enron Blame Game" was developed by David Plotz for *Slate* magazine and is found at http://www.slate.com/id/2061470/. The idea sprang from congressional testimony by Arthur Andersen representatives who blamed an accountant for document shredding and questionable accounting practices. All the finger pointing got Plotz thinking. He created this interactive information graphic that summarizes the Enron events, the players and whom they blame. The concept is simple yet the results are rather complex as you click on your favorite villain and find out who they blame for the Enron scandal. Plotz has stated, "There is an infinite chain of blame."

When involved in any type of accident or when a contract has not been completed to your satisfaction, it has become standard fare to recruit multiple defendants and not limit the blame to those obviously and directly responsible. The words foreseeable and causality are important in terms of legal liability. However, in terms of how we, as a society, view responsibility and consequently fault, is that anyone who has had anything to do with an event or accident; or could have had anything to do with it; or conceptually may have had some remote knowledge of it; or gave birth to someone who did, should be blamed.

Miss Take was in a car accident on the freeway. It had just snowed, the temperature had dropped and the snow started to freeze. She was late for a business meeting that was moved earlier at the last minute. She received a call and looked down at her cell phone on the passenger seat to see who it was. While glancing down, the car in front of her had slowed down dramatically to allow a deer to cross. Miss Take applied her brakes but, as she was driving rather closely behind the car in front of her, she failed to stop in time and hit the other car. Who's to blame? Obviously, Miss Take should probably bear some responsibility. However, who does she blame?

She blames the city who failed to hire enough people to plow the freeway; the Coordinator for Transportation and Utilities Maintenance (Snow Plow Director); the tire company who had replaced her tires; the car dealership who told her that her brakes were in good shape; the businessman who had changed their meeting time; the business colleague who had asked her yesterday to take his place at this meeting; the friend who had called her cell phone while she was driving; the city (again) for allowing deer to wander on the freeways; the Department of Natural Resources for supporting a deer population that was obviously too large; the driver of the car in front of her who failed to see the deer in time to slow down at a more appropriate rate; the manufacturer of her car who didn't design a great location to place her cell phone such that she would not have to look at the passenger seat for it. She also blames the driver of a car on the freeway on-ramp who was going so slowly that she was delayed for her appointment. If given a few more minutes to think about it, she will probably come up with some more people to blame.

When Brittany was sixteen years old she had better things to do than go to Fairfield High School and then Butler Tech. She used to skip school...a lot. Now at eighteen, Butler County Juvenile Court Judge David Niehaus blamed this on Brittany's father, Brian Gegner, and ordered him to jail for contributing to the delinquency of a minor by not following a court order that required him to be sure his daughter got her GED. It was interesting that while Brian

Gegner did have legal custody of Brittany, she was living with her mother at the time that she was truant. She told WCPO TV in May, 2008, "Of all the punishments they could have given him, to make him go to jail? I mean, probation—until I get my GED—would be reasonable, but to send him to jail? That's overboard."

So, as a parent you may be responsible for the actions of your adult children. "I'm about to be nineteen and my Dad's being punished for something I did when I was sixteen," says Brittany. "It's like I should, if anybody should be punished for this," said Brittany. Perhaps they should have also blamed some of her friends with whom she was hanging out and sent at least a few of them to jail as well. And why not send some of her teachers and school administrators to jail for failing to teach well enough to keep her interested in academics and for the inability to set up a curriculum and an educational environment that was conducive to her learning style. Please let us not forget to blame gun manufacturers and video game makers; they must have also had something to do with her lack of focus.

3. Learning to Blame

"If at first you don't succeed, blame your parents."

Marcelene Cox

How do we learn? I am a teacher and love to teach. But am I teaching principles that people already intrinsically know or are these new and foreign ideas? I teach Pharmacology (how drugs affect the body and how the body affects drugs) and Anesthesiology to medical students and other doctors. Many of these concepts are difficult to grasp and are based on advanced math and/or science. I'd like to pretend that students are learning what I'm teaching and what I'm teaching is new and exciting stuff. On the other hand, we rarely take the Blaming class in school, perhaps because it fills up so quickly? Pretty much all of us remember learning our ABCs in grade school. A, B, C = Accuse, Blame, and Criticize. We may have even learned about D, E, and F; Deny, Excuse, and Fault. We were told that we had to keep practicing these every day until we got really good at them—and we did! Many of us blame well and it seems like such a natural phenomenon. How then do we go about learning to blame? Is it part of a collective unconscious into which we can all tap? Is it an inborn and innate behavior? Or, is this simply a behavior that we learn when we are so young that it appears to be natural and innate.

Inborn or learned behavior?

From the time we are almost born, before leaving the womb, we are introduced to blames. Working as an Obstetric Anesthesiologist, I have spent much time with laboring women. The labor and delivery suite is a great place to hear blame. "You did this to me!" (Referring to the baby's father.) "It was his fault!" We hear blame frequently as newborns, infants, toddlers, and children. We seem to become proficient at blaming from a very young age. Is this because we are taught so well and it is a skill that is easy to pick up? Is it because we have such great blame teachers? Or is it because blaming is not really a learned behavior, but an innate quality? Has the blaming gene been sequenced yet by the human genome project? It wouldn't be on the Y chromosome since blaming is common to both sexes and only males have the Y chromosome. But it is so culturally and religiously diverse that it does, in a sense, appear to be an inborn trait of our species.

Indeed, we haven't evolved much beyond our ancestral cousins. Koko, a 280-pound lowland gorilla and her boyfriend gorilla Michael became famous for their ability to use sign language to describe feelings and express new ideas. One day Koko broke her toy cat. Her trainer knowingly asked her who had broken the cat and Koko casually pointed at Kate her night handler. In another instance, Michael ripped a jacket belonging to a trainer and when asked who was responsible for the incident, signed "Koko." Upon further inquiry, Michael appeared to change his mind, and indicated that Dr. Patterson, their teacher, was actually to blame, before finally confessing. The gorilla's responses seem to provide evidence of intentional deceit. Does Koko and Michael's deflecting of blame mean that this blaming ritual is so hard-wired into us as individuals that we should just learn to live with it? Or is it a behavior and attitude that we can rise above and learn to use it sparingly and wisely?

As children

Before we even develop the basic ability to speak; when our activities are limited to smiling, pooping, eating, and crying, we are still at the precognizant phase in our lives. We have no true self-identity and are heavily influenced by those around us. Parents play a significant role in shaping our behaviors. So what is it that newborns and infants hear that may help formulate their innocent minds? "Look what you did!" or "I can't believe that you did that!" may be exclaimed following a messy diaper, food thrown on the floor, or our precious baby waiting until the diaper is off before urinating like a city fountain all over your clothes. "Why can't you just sleep a little longer?" "I'm so exhausted because she never sleeps more than two hours." "I can't get any sleep because my baby is colicky." "I can't make any plans because of the baby." "I would love to… but I can't because of the baby."

These remarks do influence how this young one will behave ten years from now. If this was a scene from the movie *Look Who's Talking*, the baby may respond, "I don't even know how to roll over onto my back, I've not yet learned to speak or even crawl and I've never left my crib on my own accord. I've exhibited only natural bodily functions, yet my parents who chose to bring me into this world have blamed and accused me of making life hard for them. I know they love me but why don't they take some responsibility for my birth and behavior? What were they expecting when they had me shipped here, that I would poop flowers and spit up potpourri?"

This finger pointing not only continues but worsens as we grow from infancy through childhood. Our parents, who are often, but not always, perfect will sometimes lose their tempers. They're tired, working hard at home or at business. They had a bad day and need to "vent." So, it turns out that the toys left in the middle of the living room were the reason for my dad having a bad day at work; or "My not cleaning my room is why my mother was late for all her appointments today." Of course we can always draw lines and make connections between pretty much any two events.

Psychologists describe grandiosity and omnipotence during infancy. All infants have feelings of being able to control everything and being responsible for many facets of life outside of him or her. There is no separation between themselves and the world around them. Once they realize that they do not have control over others' behavior and over nature itself, this is a set-up for disappointment. Martha Craven Nussbaum in *Upheavals of Thought: Intelligence of Emotions*, writes, "To the extent that all infants enjoy a sense of omnipotence, all experience shame at the recognition of their human imperfection …" This shame can be healthy or unhealthy depending upon how it is received and responded to by the parents.

In *Overcoming Life's Disappointments*, Harold Kushner argues that "childish fantasy of grandiosity, being at the center of everything that happens, manifests itself in our tendency to feel guilty, to feel personally responsible every time something we were involved in doesn't work out as we had hoped."

While this may be true, we encourage our children's omnipotence and grandiose behaviors by blaming them for things that they have nothing to do with. We support the contention that it is okay to accuse others for our misgivings and bad fortune. We make them feel guilty about everything from a teacher strike to a streak of bad weather. Children are like sponges. They hear blaming all the time. They learn the good, the bad, and the ugly. We teach them to blame not only by accusing them for things that they may or may not have any control over, but also by our verbal examples. We teach that it is okay to blame our parents, our siblings, our schools, our teachers, and our bosses when we are not happy. You can blame anyone but never blame yourself. We tell kids it's their fault. But what we are really teaching them is that *"it is not our fault."*

Blame is accompanied by deception. As in the example of the two gorillas, these were not innocent accusations; there was dishonesty involved. The development of deception in children follows a similar pattern. In several interesting studies, some of which were conducted by Michael Lewis of the University of Medicine and Dentistry of New Jersey in New Brunswick, children were led into a room and asked to face one of the walls. The researcher explained that he was going to set up a toy a few feet behind them. After setting up the toy, he leaves the room and asks the child not to turn around and peek at the toy. The child is secretly filmed and then the experimenter returns and asks them whether they peeked. Most three-year-olds peek, and then half of them lie about it. By the age of five, all of them peek and all of them lie. Rather disturbing statistics. It seems that from a very young age, children can learn to mask their emotional expressions while lying. This of course carries over into adulthood where most people tell about two or more important lies each day. Children often know more than we give them credit for; they are privy to many things that others are not. They see what goes on at home and what goes on in the car. They hear what conversations you've had on the phone and in person.

Without our knowledge or consent, children pick up on our dishonest and deceptive behavior. We view our own behavior not only as quite innocent, but even, at times, positive and helpful. We make excuses to ourselves and our children for telling "white" lies, and of course blame something or someone else for "needing" to utter them.

Learning from siblings

From the youngest age, even before we have started to master our native tongue, children start to blame. Siblings are a wonderful target of blame. Many of us know how the Sibling Blame Game is played. The game is started by some kind of verbal argument or all-out fight between at least two of your children. You, the parent, get angry and tell them to "stop fighting," "no more arguing," "go to your rooms," or "both of you stop it!" Or you think ahead, take a deep breath and keep your calm. You gently remind them to "please use nice words when talking to each other." Your choice of responses is important but your behavior and teaching by example is more important. Regardless of your verbal response, you will most likely hear this answer, "Well she started it," as they point a finger toward each other. The Game is on!

While we should expect some amount of rivalry among siblings, is it normal or healthy for our kids to deflect responsibility and shift it to their brother or sister? What's remarkable when you listen to sibling blame is how fast and natural it is. Even before there is time for cognitive processing, the answer is blurted out. Before you finish saying, "hey kids," the retort has been started. "I didn't do it!" "She did it." "He did it" "They started it." "Why are you always blaming me?" This is a critical time for your children to learn proper communication and how to get along with others. These are formative years for developing socialization skills. This sibling relationship sets the stage for other relationships that will develop later in life.

It is not just your kids who feel it is appropriate to blame their siblings for everything from using up the last of the toothpaste, milk, or cereal; to stealing their clothes, toothbrush, or homework;

to drawing on the walls, not taking out the garbage, or their grades in school. In the first chapter I discussed some of the sibling rivalry in the biblical story of Jacob and Esau. Esau was the firstborn twin and his brother Jacob was born immediately afterwards, still grasping Esau's heel. His Hebrew name, Ya'akov, derives from the root for "heel." It is a belief in Jewish tradition that Jacob was trying to hold Esau back from being the firstborn, and in that way lay the claim for the Abrahamic legacy. From this we learn that sibling rivalry and the sibling Blame Game start very early in life. So early in fact that it may begin pre-birth. We can also begin to appreciate that, unlike Las Vegas, what goes on in the womb may not stay in the womb. It may have great repercussions for later in life. We now find out that this may be true even if siblings aren't twins.

David Lawson of University College in London presented a study with 14,000 families at the British Association Festival of Science in 2007. The researchers determined that children in larger families were likely to be shorter than average—about an inch shorter. Further, the firstborn is usually taller than their younger siblings. The reasons for this are not quite clear but may be related to the condition of the womb after the first pregnancy or simply because of less financial and nutritional resources for later siblings. But, the important take away message is that if you have an older sibling, you now have a scientific reason to blame them for your height and anything that may accompany the woes of your shorter stature—sports, jobs, dates, etc. Pass this one onto your friends for them to use for extra blame ammunition (blamunition) against their older siblings. The responsibility for your siblings' misfortunes wasn't just in their minds—it has some true and verifiable backing in fact. Well, this "fact" may help you to feel better in the short-term, but I contend that it gives you an "out." Like the majority of blame, it allows us to settle back and accept what we are given. We no longer bear the responsibility.

"I no longer have to try as hard because I know that it's not my fault." But where does this get you? You can put in less than 100 percent effort at playing basketball and when you don't make that important shot or sink that critical free-throw, you can blame it on your brother. Better yet, you can sit on the couch now and watch basketball on TV instead of actually playing because you know that it is your older brother's fault that you weren't taller (and probably better looking). So any attempt that you make to become highly proficient won't ever be as good as it could have been, had you been born first.

What can we do as parents to not fuel the fire of sibling rivalry? We can try not to get involved in the fight or conflict and let the children work it out. If the children know we will not step in, they will often resolve it themselves. Don't get caught in the middle. Don't take sides without knowing the whole story. Don't place blame inappropriately. Discuss appropriate behavior. Long range goals to decrease the incidence of the sibling Blame Game: Try to set a great example by not being deceptive. Encourage feelings of worth by praising children for who they are. Try not to associate who your child is with what they do. For example: "I really don't like you when you do that" should be replaced with "I really don't like when you act like that" or "I really don't like that behavior." Your dislike is for a specific behavior, not for your child.

Younger children are not always innocent and the older children are not always guilty, and vice versa. The young ones learn from us and their older siblings what pushes buttons to get reactions. Reward positive behavior and emphasize the strength of the family as a unit.

Learning from friends

As we grow older, we become proficient at transferring some of our responsibility from siblings to friends. Our children expand their horizons from a close association with their parents and siblings to a broader-based network of friends. As parents we want our children to hang out with "nice kids," "respectful kids," "sweet kids," and "smart kids." We know that our kids will be influenced in some way and so we hope that it will be a positive experience. Our first experience with our toddler children playing with other toddler children is rather similar to what they have learned with their siblings. Point to a broken toy on the ground and ask, "Who broke this?" Just as with the gorillas Koko and Michael, you'll see all arms flying outward with fingers quickly pointed at someone else in the room and everyone together in perfect harmony exclaiming, "he did it!" or "she did it!" or perhaps "I didn't do it!"

There is rarely accountability, especially if it can be easily shunted to our siblings and friends. At the next stage of their development, we find out that our children have "normal" friends and not perfect friends. Their language changes from, "Billy did it" to "Billy made me do it." Four-year-old Billy, like Superman, has suddenly taken on amazing powers. He is able to coerce other small children in a single bound. All of the lessons and values that you thought you had instilled in your children fly out the window at the first sign of their friends making a suggestion. Of course, we're just assuming that their friends are the ones that made the suggestion in the first place. These friends probably tell their parents that your child was the one that made them do the same thing.

As they grow into older children and teenagers, they are faced with new choices. As parents we feel that we are losing control over how our children dress, where they go, what they do, and with whom they do things. Kids look to friends for clues as to what is socially acceptable. They don't want to feel left out so they look to their peer group to confirm their self-worth. The peer pressure they feel is occasionally toward innocent or even positive behavior. However, often peer pressure is directed toward negative behaviors of drinking alcohol, smoking, taking drugs, or having sex. Of course we question our children about their behavior and are told, "Everyone does it this way," "Everyone went to the party," "Everyone had a drink," "Everyone wears these," "Everyone is doing *it*." I'm always afraid to know what the *it* is.

Blaming the peer group for imposing these pressures is normal and common. Is it right? Having your child/teenager explain how or why they want to change their style to fit in with what is now accepted in their social group is fine. Having your child/teenager commit an illegal act because it is what is expected in their social group is not fine. It is common practice for our children to blame peers and their social network of friends for their own disregard for previously instilled family values. This peer group not only acts to help reaffirm and accept your teenagers' actions, but may act as a social net to help support children experiencing difficulty at home. Just as in the cases of deception and blaming, you may have abandoned those social values that you were trying to inspire within your children. You taught them the words and told them that this is how to act toward others, especially family. Then they watch you fighting with your neighbors. They see you arguing with their siblings. They see you fighting or even divorcing the other parent.

Who closer in the family is there than the other parent? I'm reminded of the new, very liberal church in our town. They have only three commandments and seven suggestions. Yes, we fight and teach the children that those all-important family commandments were actually only suggestions. Now they have other suggestions from their social group. Instead of blaming their new-found behavior on our lack of ability to fulfill our promises to them, our kids blame it on "Everyone else is doing it..."

While the majority of these behavioral changes are transitory, the general principle of blaming our friends for our actions is well-learned and rarely short-lived. How many times have you gone out with one or more friends as adults and decided beforehand to not drink alcohol or not have more than one drink, or that you are going to be home at a certain hour, or not eat too much food at the party? Then, surrounded by the encouraging social network, all of your goals for the evening quickly disappeared, just like that last drink. Who do we blame—our friends and peer group or business colleagues who made it uncomfortable to not go against our values?

We also carry this phenomenon of bowing to and blaming social pressure into adulthood with our peer group now being defined as fashion magazines and trade magazines and hobby magazines. We see pictures of models, new gadgets and devices that "Everyone is using or wearing or eating or swimming in or traveling to or cutting with or creating with or listening to or watching or ..." We tell our spouse, our family, and ourselves that we *must* get this from the infomercial or from that website. We see that it is the new trend and we want to be part of it. Of course it rarely is as good as we hoped that it would be. So our response is, "But it looked so cool on TV." Let's blame the picture quality on the new 100-inch plasma screen that you also just had to have because all of your friends and neighbors were getting bigger and better TVs.

This is no different than our kids wanting or doing something that their friends have or have done. We tell them not to conform. Remember saying to them, "Just because everyone else is doing it, doesn't mean that you have to," or "Just because they did it, doesn't make it right"? So, if we've been saying the same thing over and over again and giving the same message to try to instill this behavior and attitude in our kids, how come they never learn this principle? Because they don't just hear what we're saying; they also see what we're doing. It is our fault. They see mom or dad in the cell phone store checking out all the newest devices. They see us looking with envy at our friends' new computers, or iPods, or digital cameras or televisions or cars. Then they see us get our new one. Was it out of the adult form of peer pressure? Usually. This is what we teach our children from a very young age. This helps them understand and begin to establish their own excuse network and pattern of blaming their friends, first as individuals and then later as groups of friends and peers. Just using the term peers or friends, rather than individual names, allows us to blame them more easily.

Just as the saying goes, "Well, you know what they say..." Help me out here, I'm never really sure who they are. Thus, it's easy to blame them too! The peer group pressure at your child's soccer game or at the locker or lunchroom at school may also be difficult to define and so it becomes easier to shift responsibility.

4. Why We Blame

"There can be no doubt that the average man blames much more than he praises. His instinct is to blame. If he is satisfied he says nothing; if he is not, he most illogically kicks up a row."

Arnold Bennett

The urge to blame is enormous, overwhelming, and at times overpowering. But from where does this urge initiate? Should we blame nature or blame nurture? What is it about blaming that we love? Is it something so addictive that we just can't stop doing it? Or, is everybody so at fault that it is natural to blame them, and it would be ridiculous to not take advantage of the situation? We often blame others to avoid taking responsibility. Not all blaming is bad. Blaming often stems from our unsatisfied expectations; standards that either we or society have established to help create and maintain order within our lives. If we see that something is not achieving a reasonably expected outcome *and* we can improve upon it somehow, then attributing fault may be reasonable and may prove beneficial. If a bridge collapses and we find out that building codes were violated and standards weren't met by the construction company because of loop holes in the law, making necessary changes in those laws and reinforcing building codes may prevent further disasters and save lives. This is productive root-cause analysis. This is accountability without re- vengeful blame. By rationally analyzing systems and behaviors we are more likely to be able to make improvements. The common goal is to improve safety. This is different from typical blaming, which is associated with fear, resentment, self-pity, distrust, depression, anger, and hatred - very non-productive.

Oftentimes our expectations are unreasonable. If life were perfect, what would happen? Life isn't perfect and we still establish our expectations as if it were so. This is a predestined pathway to unfilled hopes and lots of blaming.

Jack Canfield, the success Guru famous for his *Chicken Soup for the Soul* series, delineates sixty-four principles to achieve success in his book, *The Success Principles: How to Get from Where You Are to Where You Want to Be*. Responsibility is the first principle that Mr. Canfield discusses. Having responsibility is a big responsibility that many fear. As a society we focus on the negative side of most situations. Even those who view themselves as positive people shift toward the dark side when it comes to blaming. You can't blame and be positive at the same time. You can certainly achieve some short-term gains from blaming. However, the long-term implications both for you and others will not be positive.

"To err is human, to forgive is divine." If we believe this statement, then we will leave the forgiving up to God or some other divinity. If it is human nature to err and be at fault, then it also must be our human duty to blame.

Innate need

Blaming is most likely a learned behavior. However, we must consider certain facts: 1) the intense psychological drive to blame is so strong that most people are never able to stop despite multiple, sincere attempts, 2) the behavior is also seen among our primate relatives, and 3) blaming begins at a very young age, even before we develop verbal abilities. These considerations support the contention that blaming and accusing may represent innate traits of our species. Most character traits, like happiness, are about 50 percent genetically determined. So, while we are not completely sure about the origin and genetic coding for accusing, we can probably still blame genetics, at least in part, for our blaming behavior.

Copying behavior

Since blaming begins at such a young age, the earliest known blaming behaviors are probably based simply on copying. We see many examples of how our children are able to duplicate both our bad and good behavior. With repetition, infants and children improve their blaming techniques and advance their status in the Blame Game. When you watch the rapidity in which kids blame siblings and each other or even blame fantasy friends, it is clear that this does not require much cognitive processing. Initially, the finger pointing and calling out, "he did it," is a matter of closely replicating what they have witnessed multiple times by those who are close to them—us.

The reasons why we blame seem more complex as we age. Occasionally, even as adults, we may fall back on our intrinsic reflex blaming action. You may be in a business meeting and the boss angrily yells, "Who is responsible for the ideas on the last ad campaign?" Before you can even think about what you are doing or what she said, you immediately start pointing your finger at someone else; at anyone. And the first thing that comes to mind or might even be vocalized is, "he did it." There has not been enough time for you to cognitively process what has been said or done. This has become so ingrained that it would qualify as instinctive behavior. Of course if your boss came in the room for your business meeting and had a smile on her face, sat down and said with a happy tone, "Who is responsible for the ideas on the last ad campaign?" your arm and accusing finger would probably not shoot out toward your colleague. Blaming at its base may be intuitive. However, this does not mean that all blaming is purely inherent and unconscious. In fact, much blaming can and does involve deeper levels of thought, is well-rationalized and deliberate.

Avoid responsibility

The most common reason given for our blaming others for any misfortunes, misdeeds, or mistakes is our need to avoid responsibility. Everyone makes mistakes. They are impossible to avoid and while we may try to minimize their occurrences, it would be foolish to say or to hope that we will not make mistakes. It's not even worth vowing to try to make *fewer* mistakes. Nobody steps out of their house in the morning and intentionally makes mistakes.

Sometimes we are moderately unaware of our surroundings and do not exhibit adequate situational awareness, which may lead to creating mistakes. We may make mistakes because our judgment may be somewhat impaired by a lack of knowledge, misinformation, or by mind-altering agents (alcohol, etc). Blame has nothing to do with how often we make mistakes or what kind of mistakes we make. Blame only has to do with whether we are willing to take responsibility for our actions; good or bad, intentional or unintentional. Most of us easily take it for granted that we should be responsible for all of our positive actions and good deeds. Many people believe that we should only be responsible, in part, for our negative *intentional* actions. In other words, if a person intentionally harms another person through speech, action or even inaction, he or she is at fault and should take responsibility for this.

Unfortunately, very few people comprehend the importance of taking responsibility for *all* of our actions even when they turn out to be mistakes that have or appear to have negative consequences. You witness a car accident—a rear end collision. The person in the front car who was hit was stopped at a red light and wasn't even moving. Whose fault was it? Obviously, the driver of the second car. Is it reasonable to suppose that the driver of the second car hit the first car on purpose? Probably not. Therefore, it was probably, truly an accident. Does that resolve the driver of any responsibility? If I am the driver of the second car, I will immediately be able to come up with several reasons for the accident. None of which will be my fault and all of which will have been beyond my control. Since it wasn't intentional, should I not be held completely responsible? Of course if the first car was not there in the first place, an accident would not have been possible. Therefore, even though they were not moving, some would argue, that the driver of the first car, also has to take some of the blame for the accident.

Responsibility is a bitch. We try to preserve our self-esteem and our sense of self-worth by only recognizing our positive outcomes. This is a well-accepted and "normal" tool for helping us feel important or at least adequate on a daily basis. I feel stupid several times a day because there are so many things that I

The Blame Game

don't know. There are facts that I should have at the tip of my tongue; phone numbers and names that I should know like the back of my hand, locker combinations and passwords that I knew yesterday and for some reason can't recall today. Lack of focus? Distractions? Early Alzheimer's? I had someone or something in mind to blame for these memory lapses, but for the life of me I can't recall who or what it was …

We have a need to minimize our feelings of inadequacy. However, there is an interesting paradox which occurs. We feel better when we are in control of ourselves, our jobs, our families, and our destiny. People often complain that they want more control over their lives. Yet, at the first sign of trouble or a challenge, they are ready to hand their responsibility and blame off to the first person walking by.

To take responsibility for things that we've said or done that were unintentional and which directly or indirectly led to trouble or harm (i.e., a mistake), is often very difficult for many of us. Ambrose Bierce was a civil war veteran and journalist who wrote a satirical dictionary called *The Devil's Dictionary*. He referred to "responsibility" as a detachable burden easily shifted to the shoulders of God, Fate, Fortune, Luck, or one's neighbor. In the days of astrology it was customary to unload it upon a star." Unfortunately, in almost a century since these words were written, there is little change in our societal attitude about responsibility. Even the word "responsibility" carries with it negative connotations. Writer, comedian, and late night television host Bill Maher has declared, "We have the Bill of Rights. What we need is a Bill of Responsibilities." This is really unnecessary since every right is accompanied by a responsibility. The number of responsibilities that each of us have is endless. We may dream of being given more responsibility in our homes or in our jobs, but most of us don't even claim to have responsibility over things in which we are in control. We complain that we don't like our jobs because we don't control the hours or we have to work more hours than we want to. Well, you are in control! It is your decision to work that job. There are few jobs that people would consider to be "perfect." This will always give us something to complain about, but if something is important to you, you will have not just the ability, but the responsibility to change it. We can each change more facets of our lives than we give ourselves credit for. That statement is meant to be a positive affirmation. Yet when many of you read that, you want to deny its truth because it places more responsibility on your shoulders. If you're not happy with something or someone—change it!

The Greek Stoic philosopher Epictetus was born in A.D. 55 as a slave. He became free and lived in Rome until his exile to northwestern Greece. As a Stoic, he focused on improving individuals' spiritual well-being and taught that virtue was the sole good. Everything really good or really bad that happened in a person's life depended only upon them. Clear judgment and inner calm were developed through the practice of logic, reflection, and concentration. Epictetus stated, "God has entrusted me with myself." This is one of our primary responsibilities. Yet we tend to shift responsibility to others; to heredity; and to our environment. We view our limitations, either real or imaginary, as being beyond our control. We can find stress relief by failing to claim responsibility.

Albert Ellis, the American Psychologist who founded Rational Emotive Behavior Therapy (REBT) in the 1950s, believed that "the best years of your life are the ones in which you decide your problems are your own. You do not blame them on your mother, the ecology, or the president. You realize that you control your own destiny."

When I was a young child, I crashed my bike into a mailbox. I had learned the power of the pedals but had not yet appreciated the benevolence of the brakes. I brought my bike up to the house to show my father. Holding up the bike, I said, "It broke." My father listened patiently and nodded. He then responded that he would know when I was mature when I would take responsibility for the bike and state, "I broke it." When we stop saying "It got lost," "It broke," "It tore" and instead say "I lost it," "I broke it," "I tore it." The "it" refers to an inanimate object for which I have claimed the right and responsibility to use or wear. Responsibility shouldn't end with the first time that I have a problem with the object. I want to maintain my right but have given up my responsibility. "It" now takes on a life of its own; "it" is responsible for "itself" and can now legitimately be blamed.

Until we have learned to appreciate ourselves despite our frailties and mistakes, we will not be able to take on the honor of being responsible for ourselves, our possessions, and our actions.

Internalize versus externalize

Internalizing and externalizing is an interesting psychological phenomenon. In academia it is known as fundamental attribution error. When we see someone doing something that we have determined is bad, mean, wrong, hurtful, or disrespectful in some way, we internalize a reason for this. When *we* do something that is bad, mean, wrong, hurtful, or disrespectful in some way to others, we search externally for a reason. When we think about others and try to attribute causes for their actions, we internalize the cause by making assumptions regarding their personality, their values, their disposition, and their motivations. In this way we are able to more completely and justifiably blame them for their actions without having to invoke a third party. We might find ourselves committing a similar act in which we are not proud, such as maneuvering our way into a parking spot that someone else had been waiting for or not answering the phone when we know who is on the other end. How do we handle this? By creating an external motive for our actions. We blame something or someone else for either making us do this thing or for creating an environment in which we are forced to act badly. We might exclaim, "I would never have done that, except that I'm late for picking up my kids at school."

We acknowledge that we are intrinsically good people who would not knowingly be mean or disrespectful to others. So when we find ourselves involved in a negative behavior, we do our best to attribute it to a third, uninvolved party. We again play the Blame Game and recruit others to explain our unwarranted behavior.

When faced with describing "bad" behavior or attributing causes, we claim knowledge of motives and personalities for people that we've never met. Similar to blaming, attributing negative motivation to someone else also makes us feel superior to those individuals. But this feeling doesn't get us anywhere or help us learn or grow to be better people or help us to understand one another. We walk around with more negative thoughts, which become negative words, which intentionally or unintentionally become negative actions.

Wrong focus

We each have preconceived notions about what the world should be like; what our life should be like; what our day should be like, and what everybody should or shouldn't be doing or saying. We get frustrated when things don't turn out the way that we believe they are "supposed" to be. We tell ourselves, "That was supposed to be faster or slower, or better, or smoother, or …" "He should have been nicer or funnier, or smarter, or earlier, or later, or …" "It should be better or bigger, or higher, or smaller, or …" "He should have moved the car or thrown out those papers, or finished the drywall, or packed up the clothes, or started playing, or …" When we assess the events that occur and add our belief system to those events, we create a sense of discontentment. We get frustrated not because of what actually happened but because we incorrectly placed our expectations and focus on what happened.

When things didn't go as we planned, we play the Blame Game and accuse those involved for not following our mysterious plan. Maybe we blame the weather or Mother Nature or God. Rather than trying to see the other side of a story or realize that sometimes things don't happen the way that we believe that they should, we blame.

I was teaching a martial arts class and Steve was one of my advanced students. One day shortly after starting the class, Steve walked in late. I told him to "quickly join the class." The class was in the middle of doing some kicks and punches and I noticed that Steve had forgotten much of what he had been taught and looked uncomfortable. After correcting him several times and commenting on his poor technique, I mentioned how he needed to have better focus. He quietly leaned over to me and asked, "Do you think that I'm Steve?"

"Yes, of course," I replied. He continued, "I'm Brad, Steve's twin brother. Steve told me to try the class out. I've never done this

The Blame Game

before."

Perhaps we are basing our ideal of what "should" happen on erroneous information. Perhaps as with my error with Steve, there is a case of mistaken identity. What are the chances of that happening? Well, they are not zero, because it did happen and I was caught blaming based on my assumptions and incorrect information. Sometimes we hear things that we misinterpret or we don't hear the whole story and we make up the rest. We are sure that we have the facts straight and are justified in our blame. Then we learn more about the story, find out that there was information that we were not privy to that completely changed the outcome and we now must remove the blame. We believe in "should"s and "could"s, which leads to frustration and blaming others for not achieving our goals. This also prevents us from dealing with our feelings or dealing with the situation and trying to correct any issues.

Rational Emotive Behavioral Therapy (REBT) posits that people have irrational and rigid beliefs. Irrational beliefs result in low frustration tolerance, people deprecation, and overgeneralizations. When people use rigid "should"s, "must"s, and "ought"s, they disturb and upset themselves. It is our nature to think, that "the conditions under which I live absolutely MUST, at practically all times, be favorable, safe, hassle-free, and quickly and easily enjoyable, and if they are not that way it's awful and horrible. Living within this framework leads to frustration and discomfort, intolerance of others, self-pity, anger, depression, and blaming. This mindset is also associated with behaviors such as procrastination, avoidance, and inaction.

Suicide is 70 percent more likely among male physicians in the United States than among other professionals, and 250 to 400 percent higher among female physicians. On average, the United States loses the equivalent of an entire medical school class each year to suicide. Depression affects about 12 percent of males and 18 percent of females, but among medical students and residents, the rate may be as high as 30 percent. After accidents, suicide is the most common cause of death among medical students. Why? Physicians are "wounded healers." They have early personal experiences with loss, traumas, and family conflicts while growing up that has attracted them to the medical profession. Some blame genetics, previously undiagnosed mental illness, or a perfectionist attitude that sets up an environment of guilt and self-recrimination. For a detailed look at problems in Perfectionism see Harvard Professor Dr. Tal Ben-Shahar's new book *The Pursuit of Perfect*. Still others blame the rigorous work-load, nights on call, lack of sleep, and the stress of taking care of very sick patients. The medical profession is a stressful job with irregular hours.

My thoughts: There are some medical students who have wanted to be doctors since the time they were born— before they had any realistic idea of what being a doctor involved; there are other medical students who did not decide to become physicians until young adulthood or even after attempts at other careers. The "always wanted to be a doctor" types have not gone through an adult-level of self-assessment regarding their chosen career. They are focused on the prize (graduation), not the journey (medical school). They are continuously told that it will get easier—but it doesn't. Then they are told that it will be easier after they graduate. Yet, after graduation is internship. They are now physicians with life and death decisions, long hours, and little control over scheduling, grueling and/or boring rounds while sleep-deprived and the imposing realization that "this is what I have been working toward for the past four years. It may never get any better than this. What was I thinking?" Of course this is depressing!

Everyone who has gone to medical school knows someone or knows of someone who attempted or committed suicide during internship year. Most of those interns felt both depressed about their situation and limited by their options. Their options obviously were not limited, they were under complete control, but sometimes this control is not apparent.

It's easier

Guns
Video

games TV
Violence
Hip Hop
Rock Videos

These are just a few of the objects and activities that we blame for societal problems. Many of us join suit with the media when it starts to play the Blame Game and its need for finger pointing whenever a crime occurs. We spend little time discussing the psyche of the person who committed the crime and look for bigger and better explanations. We want global reasons to explain behavior. We want a scapegoat to be able to excuse our actions and bad behaviors. If the crime was gun-related, of course we blame the gun laws, and the people who made the gun laws, and the people who make the guns and sell the guns, and the people who make the bullets.

The fact that someone decided to use the gun in a bad way is almost ignored. When the crime consists of violence, we try to determine if the criminal was playing too many video games, or watching too much violence on TV, or grew up in a violent home, or involved in hip hop or gangsta rap culture. For sex crimes, we can blame hip hop, gangsta rap and rock videos, for drug crimes we can blame hip hop, gangsta rap and "inner city" culture. For violence at high schools and colleges, let's blame violent video gaming.

We have a societal desire to excuse personal behavior and responsibility. This is not to say that people, especially children, are not influenced by what they see and hear or that violence on television, videos, and as promoted by hip hop music, is healthy or beneficial for society. But are we to blame these *things* for individual's wrong-doings? It's easier and more satisfying to blame an industry, especially one such as hip hop, than to limit our liability to a single individual (a uniblamer). But, where does that end? Should we stop the production of all movies that discuss or show any fighting or violence? How about war documentaries? Should they be outlawed? Are they any less violent in their portrayal than what is frequently described in many songs or displayed in video games? Who is to decide the standards? When pre-teens start to wear skimpy, inappropriate clothing and wear outrageous hairstyles, we don't blame the teen. We shift the blame to their parents, Britney Spears, Jessica Simpson, Lindsey Lohan, and the music video industry. If playing video games is the cause of one person's violent rage at a local high school, why haven't all the kids playing these video games shown similar attitudes and aggressive behavior? The answer is that it is not the video games that are to blame. It is the person committing the act.

Blaming and then banning all video games or having someone creating minimal violence standards so that no one is exposed to any computer-animated aggression will not eliminate violence in our society. But it will take away freedoms of the creators, producers, marketers, and viewers, in addition to teaching our children that they don't have to take responsibility for their actions. Act badly and blame Tupac.

All of that said, I do believe that improving the messages delivered by the hip hop culture, improving the role of women in rock videos, decreasing senseless violence in video gaming, and getting parents to be more actively involved in their children's lives should be encouraged through education and creating a sense of societal pride. Everyone who solicits the business of industries that support or encourage violence is responsible for their purported influence. I am not a fan of the senseless violence and flagrant sex that is encouraged by certain music cultures. However, neither I nor my children have ever committed any crimes that I am aware of because of its influence. We can choose not to listen and not to purchase. The laws of supply and demand will prevail.

Afraid of success

We poke fun at celebrities and Hollywood stars. We heavily criticize Bill Gates and "the Donald" and others who have found a way to realize huge financial accomplishments. Yet we know that it is not easy. We appreciate that with these achievements comes responsibility and liability that we are not so ready to adopt as our own. Why do so many of us want to work for others rather than manage or own a business? We can provide reasons or excuses or blame someone or something for never having had the opportunity. We complain about our bosses. But would you want their job? When you eventually get to the top of the food chain, who is there left to blame? Blame the boss. You are the boss. So let's blame the workers. Well, that may be good for your short-term ego boost, but it's disastrous for your company. Playing the Blame Game instead of taking responsibility and taking corrective actions is the formula for being downsized or going bankrupt.

If you play the role of middle management, you are lucky enough to have co-workers, inferiors and superiors. In other words, you get blamed from both ends of the corporate ladder as well as from your colleagues. The more successful you are in the corporate world, the more personal liability, accountability, and responsibility you take on. There are management consultants who are able to examine the internal success of a company by the direction in which blame flows. If blame flows upward toward management, the conclusion can be made that higher level personnel at the company are willing to take responsibility for mistakes made at lower levels of the company. If blame appears to trickle downward, the conclusion is that upper management is not willing to assume accountability and the working personnel is usually under fire; a formula for not doing well in the corporate world. As a society we have a fictional, dreamy view of the beauty and wonders of being successful. Yet we know and fear the increased internal and external stresses that are associated with these successes.

Bilbo Baggins, the famous hobbit created by J.R.R. Tolkien, lived his very comfortable life in stasis. No stairs to climb, perfectly round doors, and a lot of comfort. Every day was similar and easy. Sounds great, but he was living in fear. Like many of us, Bilbo feared change. It wasn't until Gandalf the Wizard set him in motion on his journey that Bilbo becomes enlightened and energized. Along the way, Bilbo blames Gandalf for disturbing his peaceful life; for putting him in danger. Bilbo learns to take risks and conquers his fears. He takes responsibility for himself and others and finds that he has the fortitude to succeed, emerging as the hero, free from blame.

Why do we fear success? Some have feelings of low self-esteem and lack self-worth. Others fear that they won't be able to sustain the increased demands—whatever they do will never be enough; they will risk losing it all. Still others convince themselves that success won't be worth the effort. Should I be expected to credit someone with my success just because I was planning on blaming them for my failure? As a success coach, Jack Canfield has pointed out it is rare to find people at a company who approach their most successful coworkers and ask how they are making good things happen. The desire for success is not typically as strong as the fear of rejection.

Our failures are typically shared phenomena. We are quite willing to invite our family, friends, loved ones, and business associates to our blame party to wallow in our failures. However, our successes are private and done in a vacuum without assistance. If we are willing to blame others for our losses, we should be willing to credit them with our gains.

Programmed to accept the negative

People are born and reared with an uncanny ability to remember negative events in their lives. Feeling comfortable accepting negative consequences fits in with our general scheme of shifting our responsibility to others. Looking at the world through a negative image view-finder is conducive to blaming both ourselves and others. We might talk about how great it would be to have things work out in a positive way; how wonderful it would be to win that lottery, or to get that job promotion, or to just have all the kids ready to go to school on time. But we accept negative results because it's a lot less work, time, effort, and energy.

Sit back, relax, and don't take control or responsibility for your life and negative things will happen automatically. Making positive changes in your life takes time, energy, and mental toughness. This isn't to say that you shouldn't sit back and relax, meditate, and be at peace with yourself, which I believe everyone should also do. "Good things come to those who wait?" "Patience is a virtue?" Yes. But if you are waiting for someone else to do your share of the work, or you are waiting for a stranger to drop off a check for your mortgage payment, or for the one-arm bandit in Las Vegas to pay off the jackpot, then you may be out of luck. Inactivity and failing to control your life is different than the virtue of "patience."

Thinking positively, feeling positively, and behaving positively are hard work. If you haven't tried it before, give it a shot. It's not how we were brought up or how our society functions. We have a society built on negative foundations. We have a community built on blame. Expecting the negative allows me to prepare the perfect blame in advance for why things won't work out in my favor. Impromptu blaming can be quite a challenge and even sometimes embarrassing. This situation, of not having a good blame quickly enough, can be avoided by planning for the negative and setting up your blame plan well ahead of time.

The novelist James Branch Cabell was quoted as saying, "The difference between the optimist and the pessimist: the optimist proclaims that we live in the best of all possible worlds and the pessimist fears this is true." They both live in the same world. So how could they have such different beliefs? Viewpoints have little to do with what is outside ourselves and much more to do with what is inside each of us. From a lookout on the freeway, the view of a snow-covered mountain may be a beautiful, breathtaking sight or a huge obstacle to my getting home. It is the same mountain; the only difference is my internal viewpoint. In the first view, I may thank God or the Universe for providing this natural wonder. In the second view, I might blame God or the Universe for this awful curse. Seeing life through negative, closed eyes enhances our ability to blame. It allows us to truly focus on everything that we deem "bad" and then try to pick a victim or object or event to which we can assign liability.

We ignore positive events that occur, or we are able to reframe and reinvent the occurrence in a negative way to be able to look for blame. This is closely related to our fear of accomplishment. We become adept at reformulating everything that happens to us or around us in a negative manner. In part we accomplish this feat through over-generalizations; giving greater power and importance to minor events. Rational emotive behavior therapy uses the term "awfulizing," which is a mental magnification of the importance of an unwanted situation to the level of a catastrophe.

We elevate the rating scale for an insignificant event from bad to intolerable; positive events become inconsequential. We get easily frustrated when we perceive that something will be too difficult, painful, or tedious for us to accomplish. We focus on potential difficulties and exaggerate these qualities beyond our ability to cope. How rare is it to overhear a conversation between two people where they are complimenting a third person who is not present? How often do we get the privilege of listening in to the Blame Game where a third party is an absentee blamee? Gossip is the ultimate in negative speech and action. It is never helpful, and always in some way hurtful. The walls do have ears! Gossip and blaming are quite comfortable bedfellows. It is impossible to gossip without blaming somebody for something.

5. How We Blame

"It's not whether you win or lose, it's how you place the blame."

Oscar Fingal O'Flahertie Wills Wilde

In 2007, Steven Paglierani, an expert on Emergence Personality Theory, wrote an online article (http://humanistic-emergence.gaia.com/blog) entitled, "Should Therapy Encourage People to Blame?" Paglierani asserts, "If we can learn to do this then blame becomes something wonderful; a genuinely spiritual healing agent." Paglierani states that blame exists in three varieties: 1) *Excusing Blame*: we ask punishing questions and try to explain why someone was stupid and wrong; 2) *Time Limited Blame*: we dream up temporary suffering we'd like to have thrown back at them, for what we are going through; 3) *Punishing Blame*: we come up with eternal damnations for the blamees.

The types of blames in this chapter are user-friendly. I would be surprised if you have not used all of these at some time; however, some of the names may not be well-known to you. So how do we blame? Unintentionally, Subtly, Blatantly, Casually, Secretly, and Deceitfully. My goal is to briefly familiarize the reader with some interesting blaming idioms including: the slide (slang for Subtle Blaming); the bounce, burp, cough, or hiccough (terms frequently used to describe Unintentional Blaming); the blitz or the stealth (very similar to a Secret Blame but performed quickly and quietly).

There are various regional expressions that describe certain types of blames. For example, if you were on the West Coast you might have a successful evening of "rubber backing," while on the East Coast this would be described as "a spit." These are both common colloquial terms for Deceitful Blaming. In the Midwest there is no slang term for Deceitful Blaming because the Midwest Blaming Society has claimed that Deceitful Blaming is so infrequent in this area of the country that there is no need for such phrases. This being said, it is known in the underground that Deceitful Blaming is indeed performed in all areas of the country; Midwestern practitioners often refer to this style as getting in a "New Yorker" or a "Californian."

A curious term used only in Wisconsin, "the bubbler," is used to describe a Blatant Blame. In the Southwest, when you overhear that a blamer has just "taken a walk," it means that they just performed a Casual Blame (of note, this is not dissimilar from an Australian "walkabout"). This section describes styles that are nationally accepted by the International Blaming Federation.

Unintentionally

Especially for many easy blames, we no longer have to think about the reason for the blame, formulating the blame, or who should be the target of the blame. Some may be quite adept at absent-mindedly forming an entire Chain-of-Blame (CoB) without consciously processing the information. Bruce Lee, the Kung Fu master, was my martial arts inspiration growing up and is famous for the quote:

> Before I learned the art, a punch was just a punch, and a kick, just a kick. After I learned the art, a punch was no longer a punch, a kick, no longer a kick. Now that I understand the art, a punch is just a punch, and a kick is just a kick.

So it seems to be with blaming. When we are young it comes very naturally to us, we can almost blame without thinking. A blame is just a blame. A blame by any other name...Anyone, even a non-verbal child, can do it. But after growing up a little and being faced with more responsibilities in life, we find that there's a lot more to blaming than we ever would have imagined. Blaming haphazardly will work for you most of the time, but it may not always get you

The Blame Game

out of trouble or adequately shift responsibility out of your way.

Now you have to sit and think of another set of better blames; more difficult after an unsuccessful blame. This set-back could have been avoided by either more careful blame planning or becoming more proficient in blaming. Here is where you find out how much more there is to forming and delivering a Championship Blame. Shouting out, "he did it!" may work for you most of the time, but it will not always get you out of those tough situations that make the difference between "your fault" and "their fault." This is where you take apart the essence of blaming and fully, truly, deeply understand what it means to form the perfect blame.

It goes without saying that everyone's eventual goal is to become a BlameMaster®. Once you achieve this level of accomplishment, you become blaming, and blaming becomes you. Blaming will become an extension of your thoughts, feelings, and actions. You will radiate with the inner glow of being blameless. This—a total lack of responsibility for yourself and your fellow man, and a complete disrespect for the value of others—is not easily achieved. It is difficult, but it can be accomplished with regularly scheduled blaming practices and a dedicated belief in the Power of Blame.

You're driving to work, the radio is on quietly because you are talking on your cell phone and not paying quite enough attention to what you should be doing. The car in front of you suddenly stops and by the time you see it and jam on your brakes, your coffee cup flies from its holder and splashes to the floor. As this is happening your heart rate is skyrocketing, and without fully processing the information, you are yelling in slow motion at the car in front of you, "Damn you for stopping, you b∞s¥€βd!"

A Reflex Blame. You really have no idea what transpired to lead the car in front of you to stop. In fact, he didn't suddenly stop at all. You were too busy to notice that he was slowing down because the light had turned yellow and someone was crossing the road. You were also too distracted to realize that you were driving way too close to the car in front of you. But that doesn't really matter.

What matters is that you got the blame in and it was a great emotional release from the mental stress and anxiety of the near accident. You didn't even have to think about it—it just happened. Whose fault is it that you blamed the other driver instead of taking responsibility for the coffee spill yourself? You could say, "It's not my fault, the blame just happened, naturally, unintentionally."

During Unintentional Blaming, there may be little cognitive processing accompanying the blame. It just happens. You can relate this to getting your knee struck by the doctor's reflex hammer. The doctor strikes your patella tendon below the kneecap, which stretches the quadriceps tendon. This stimulates receptors to send an impulse along the femoral nerve to the spinal cord. There, the sensory nerve meets up with a motor nerve that sends an impulse back to the quadriceps muscle in your thigh, causing a contraction and your lower leg kicks out. You have very little control over this monosynaptic reflex arc. There is even an inhibitory nerve that causes the hamstring muscles in the back of the thigh to not put up a fight, so that you can kick faster and stronger. When we say that something occurs so naturally and quickly that it is just a reflex, the patellar reflex is what we have in mind.

We often think of blaming in this same frame of reference—like a monosynaptic reflex arc over which we have no control. Rather than an immediate leg kick, blaming instantaneously gets us anxious, upset, and increases our heart rate and blood pressure. We reflexively blame. There is another phenomenon that occurs with the patellar tendon response that also applies to blaming. When you focus on the reflex response, you can actually inhibit it. Being fully aware of and anticipating the reflex response is enough to diminish or completely inhibit it. As with blaming, when we interject our thoughts and consciously seek to understand a given situation, we are much less likely to blame others. We may cognitively inhibit the blame reflex by being more aware of our actions. Finally, this conscious inhibition of the reflex may be blocked by performing the Jendrassik maneuver in which you interlock fingers and hands together while the patella tendon is hit. Again, there is concordance with the blaming reflex. Even if I am consciously aware that I am ultimately at fault for a certain situation that occurred, if I get distracted by other thoughts, events, or actions, I will blame anyone or anything that comes to mind at the time that the response is needed. The act of becoming distracted in- creases the chance of both a brisk patellar response and a rapid, unplanned blame.

Subtly

In general, there is not much that is subtle about blaming. We make it a big deal, so blaming subtly and discreetly will typically not be second nature. It is a precious quality that some are born with, while in others it must be nurtured. Subtle Blaming is the antithesis of Unintentional Blaming. It is calculated and precise. Unless you are highly skilled in the Art of Blaming, it is not an accident or a reflex. It is well-planned and goal-driven. A Subtle Blame is often spoken softly and sometimes in confidence. It is best delivered when you can count on that confidence being broken quickly to pass the blame on to a broader audience without you having to repeat the blame to multiple parties.

Subtle Blames can be very successful at removing attention from ourselves and helping others focus on things or people or events that are totally unrelated to the cause of any problems. If one is proficient in Subtle Blaming, there does not even need to have been an initiating event to cause the blame. The goal in this case is to attract attention toward something or someone and not necessarily away from you. It is best accomplished in a way that the listener is able to contribute and may even believe that he or she has come up with the idea themselves. This is how the blame is propagated as the listener has a sense of ownership to the blame and wants to see it develop from its infancy.

Frank has been spending a lot of time playing basketball and then staying up late playing X-Box. He has not been able to focus well or sometimes can't even stay awake in school. Last night he forgot that he had any homework until just before his bedtime. His mother, Stephanie, spends a lot of time trying to help him do his homework, but to no avail. The problem was that he was not even sure what the assignment was; he didn't write it down and it was too late to call a friend. Frank's teacher had spoken with him and his mother several times about his attitude and behavior in class. Today, Stephanie knows that he will be in trouble for not completing his homework again. After dropping Frank off at school, she mingles with a few mothers of kids from different classes and quietly opens the discussion with, "I can't believe the homework that Mrs. Carlson has been giving the sixth-graders. I tried to help Frank with it last night but I couldn't understand it myself. We worked on it for several hours and still didn't get it finished. What does she expect of these kids?" This was just enough of a Subtle Blame to get the word spreading that sixth-grade teachers have unrealistic expectations of their students and that there is, in general, too much homework given out in school these days. Good; no one is talking about Frank's grades in school or the fact that his mother can't pull him away from his X-Box. The mission was a success; quiet dissatisfaction has been initiated about Mrs. Carlson, teachers in general, homework, and public schools. Stephanie can find comfort that both she and Frank have been relieved of responsibility.

Often a Subtle Blame is delivered without ever using the word "blame." Instead, words such as "fault," "mistake," "blunder," "responsibility," and "liability" get the point across more gently. Subtle Blames are often accompanied by terms such as "if only...", "because of the...", and "I would have but...". Subtle Blames are often delivered by candidates running in elections for public office. It is considered inappropriate and negative campaigning to use Blatant Blames against opposing candidates; yet well-prepared Subtle Blames may strikingly resonate with the audience and be more difficult to retaliate against. Subtle Blames are reminiscent of a comedian telling a great joke. The exact same joke told by someone else may not hit home; "It's all in the delivery." One of the goals of the Subtle Blamer is to not get accused of blaming. Thus, these clandestine accusations must be well camouflaged.

Blatantly

"I can't hold back!" This is in your face blaming in its purest form. "What a nerve!" "Why did he do that?" "Why did she say that?" "How come he didn't..." "Why aren't they..." "I can't believe that they ...!" There is nothing private, discreet, or subtle about this form of blaming.

Blatant Blaming is usually associated with more immediate anger and frustration. Similar to what may occur with Unintentional Blames, Blatant Blaming may be performed simply as a reflex. This style of blaming, however, is not gentle. It is often delivered in a loud and forwardly accusing manner. A Blatant Blame is direct, to the point, and it is typically very explicit. Blatant Blames are usually limited to a particular situation or occurrence.

Blatant Blaming does not usually serve any hidden purpose; the intention is most frequently to accomplish a quick fix—a rapid responsibility shift. Sometimes the motivation for this specific type of blaming is the result of unchecked revenge. When this is the case, the blame is rarely well-developed in substance or content. It merely contains the bare bones essential ingredients necessary to develop and deliver the blame. Unlike many forms of accusations, blatantly blaming is often delivered directly to the recipient, as opposed to being spread indirectly via word of mouth.

Casually

The Casual Blame is nothing fancy. It is the most commonly delivered blame nationwide. In 2006, the International Blaming Federation presented some interesting data at their annual convention. The average adult yields 3.4 blames per hour throughout the day. Obviously there were marked decreases in the blaming rate between the hours of midnight and 6:00 a.m., although the rate did not go to zero even while people were asleep. This blaming rate would predict that there are approximately 1.7 billion blames per minute or 286,426 blames every second of every day. As 63.7 percent of all documented blames have been determined to be of the "Casual" variety, this translates to a Casual Blame rate of over 182,450 per second. If there are inaccuracies in these reported data, don't blame me. As the saying goes, 97.5 percent of all data are made up. In case that wasn't clear, let me restate this fact because it is important: 98.1 percent of all data is completely fictitious.

As the name implies, you don't have to get dressed up to deliver a "Casual." No suit and tie—no long gown. In presenting a Casual Blame, one may try to recruit others, such as coworkers or friends for assistance. The Casual Blame may be delivered directly to the blamee, a representative, or anyone else who is willing to listen. The Casual Blame, unlike the "Blatant," does not imply any malice and is not typically associated with overt anger, rage, resentment, or frustration. This form of blaming is often performed "just to pass the time away" and many casual blamers do not even recognize that they were engaged in a casual blaming activity. Many casual blamers deny that what they had said was actually a blame. They felt that it was "just part of the story" or that "because it was a fact, it wasn't really a blame."

The Casual Blame is most often inserted into personal stories and frequently used in a historical sense. In other words, the event or situation that generated the blame may have transpired at any time in the near or distant past. In fact, Casual Blames are most often *not* based on active or ongoing processes. Casual Blames are also very useful for describing historical events or events in which the blamer has very little knowledge and little to no involvement. The Casual Blame is often referred to as "the innocent" because there is often no harmful intent by the blamer. The Casual Blame may be used to simply describe activity; that there is a blame inserted is almost incidental. Casual blamers are often nice people.

Secretly

The Secret Blame is often confused with the Subtle Blame; however, there are some very significant differences. Subtle Blame may be spoken anywhere: in private, in public, or delivered to national audiences via television. Whereas Secret Blames begin as confidential narratives. The "Secret" may be blatantly delivered or more delicate in its message and content. It may be pre-arranged or spontaneous. In contrast, the Subtle Blame must be well-prepared in advance, so as to disguise the very fact that this is blame. Anyone can deliver a Secret Blame well, but to produce an excellent Subtle Blame really requires a BlameMaster® or perhaps a Blame Stylist®.

Why would someone want to create a Secret Blame? What

is the impetus for generating this type of blame? There are two classic reasons for a Secret Blame and both involve anonymity. You either want everyone to know something but don't want to be associated with the accusation or you have no idea who is at fault but you want to take the first step to make sure that your name is not at the top of the list of responsible parties. Let's look at each of these types of Secret Blames.

Don't think about a purple elephant. Yes, that's right. I said, "Don't think about a great big, purple elephant!" What are you thinking about right now? The purple elephant! Once the words are in your head, it's almost impossible to ignore them. So it is with the "Secret." When you hear, "I've got a secret," the first thing we need to do is find out the secret. The simple use of the word "secret" encourages inquiry. Our nature is to discover, and a secret is something hidden, something forbidden, and something unknown waiting to be realized. If I have a blame that I would like to have propagated, but don't necessarily want to be the one to do the spreading, I suggest that I have a secret, and the need to hear it dramatically increases. The owner and originator may or may not be associated with the blame. Yet the clandestine goal is actualized when the blame makes its way around the office, the community, the school, or the church. In addition to wanting anonymity, our goal in submitting this blame is to minimize our workload. The "Secret" is a self-propagating, energy-generating phenomenon. A Secret Blame is also like playing the telephone game. The telephone game (or "broken telephone") is where a person thinks of a phrase or sentence and whispers it to someone. Each participant secretly whispers the same phrase that they just heard to the next successive player. Errors from mishearing snowball and often result in the final sentence being markedly different from the original phrase. So it is in the Secret: as it passes from one ear to the next, errors accumulate and the more inflammatory it becomes.

I'm in grade school and I pass on a tiny Secret Blame to a friend about my sister having trouble waking up this morning for school, almost making us late. Two hours later, the whole school is talking about her urinary incontinence, sleepwalking, disobedience at home, that she is always late for school, and how lazy she is.

Minimal effort, maximum retribution; and I can honestly state that I didn't say any of those nasty things about my darling sister.

Another reason for developing the Secret Blame is that I am really not sure who did it, but it wasn't me and I need people to know that. Thus, the primary goal is to avoid rather than specifically accuse; but as a means to this end, I must plant an accusational seed, water it, wait for the roots to take hold and then sit back to watch it grow. The copier at the office is broken and I use it more than anyone else. I'm not sure who broke it, but I want everyone to know that it wasn't me. It seems ridiculous to pass on a rumor that "it wasn't me who broke the copier." So instead, I attach the name of someone in the office who is likely to be at fault. I can deliver this blame in a blatant or subtle fashion since the main purpose isn't to attack someone else but to proactively defend myself. I might start the rumor that, "I heard that Jane was a real klutz in her last job and was always braking things. Looks like she might be at it again …" Or I might be more subtle, stating, "Isn't it great how Jane has really been working hard lately. She seems to be doing a lot of copying …" This will now be the talk of the office. Heat's off me; responsibility shift achieved!

Deceitfully

Unfortunately, for the recipients, Deceitful Blames are relatively common. So common in fact that Noel Coward, the award-winning playwright, actor, and composer, wrote, "it's discouraging to think how many people are shocked by honesty and how few by deceit." Similarly, Eric Blair, better known as George Orwell, stated, "In times of universal deceit, telling the truth will be a revolutionary act." The "Deceit," colloquially referred to as the "Big D," has malicious intentions. It is usually delivered to inflict damage or harm to someone. Deceits are often subtle in form although they certainly have had successes when delivered in a blatant manner.

Many people who perform Deceitful Blames are quite successful at fooling themselves into believing that they are not actually engaged in this activity. This occurs for one of three reasons: There's a hint of reality or some possible truth in the story and the blamer reasons that they are simply completing an unfinished project; 2) The blamer focuses on the prize at the end of the rainbow and they lose sight of the fact that they have wrongly accused; 3) The blamer justifies the blame because he or she felt that they were so wronged in the past.

It is hard for people to admit to being involved in a Big D because the blamer knows that they are not truthful. They want something very badly: material goods, property, people, money, or revenge. Except in extreme cases of manic behavior or overt psychosis, there is always a secondary gain associated with the Deceitful Blame. Using a Deceitful Blame against someone you have never met and someone who has no association with you would be rather pointless.

In many varieties of blaming, the blamer desires to shift responsibility away from them. A Deceitful Blame goes a step farther where the user's goal is to self-endorse and/or do harm to another party. Here are some examples of when Deceitful Blames are useful: looking for a job promotion or attempting to move up the corporate ladder; in the throes of a painful divorce and wanting more time with the kids; want to return a product for which you had buyer's remorse; just got into a car accident and you know it was your fault but there were no other witnesses; your younger sibling has always been mom and dad's favorite and you need some extra nurturing. There are many opportunities for producing Deceitful Blames. The trick is to not get caught. Although these blames involve fabrication, the desire is so strong that it often becomes believable, even to the blamer.

Most of us would berate and despise someone engaged in a Deceit Blame, yet in the right circumstances many of us have knowingly or "unknowingly" created these types of blames. If the "Deceit" is very blatant and there is knowingly no truth whatsoever connected with the blame, then there is often a great deal of anxiety associated with telling the blame and as such it may not be delivered as forcefully as it was initially intended. If, however, we have convinced ourselves that this blame may actually be true, then we can be very steadfast in our belief and the blame becomes very aggressive.

Coincidently, divorce, which is one of the more popular venues for delivering a Big D, has also been referred to as the "Big D." This has been the source of last year's controversial article in *Blamers Quarterly*, "Feeling Good About Having Double Big D's." This article discussed how to use Deceitful Blames to your advantage in a divorce. You are working late at the office, lose track of time and you're late picking up the kids from their mother's house. You know this will be an issue in the custody battle because you've been late several times before. So, you come up with a story about a traffic accident (that never occurred) or make up a tale about a previous discussion earlier in the week (that never happened) in which their mother asked that you pick them up an hour later than usual. This little "white blame" is certainly justified in your mind because we're talking child custody and how much time you get to spend with your kids.

You are in the process of divorce. Your children attend hockey lessons while they are under your care. Their father is a little too lenient at home; he lets the children stay up late and they question his authority. During the custody battle, the father blames their mother for taking them to hockey lessons which, he claims, have left the children with violent tendencies and subsequent behavioral problems. The potential secondary gain is incredible: more time with your children. When confronted with this blame, the father may very well deny that he has created a Big D. To him, the children have not been acting the way that they used to when they were all living at the same house. That was before they got into hockey. So, it only makes sense that this is the source of their behavioral troubles and disobedience.

Even successful "Deceits" are rarely satisfying types of blames because in your core, there is awareness that we have not been completely honest. We hate to admit this, and rather than take responsibility, we will even blame another person for "making us" create a Deceitful Blame. "If she hadn't done this or he hadn't done that, I wouldn't have had to say those things." We may reason that it is justified because this will be better for the kids in the long-term. We can do the same thing when we use deceit in the corporate world. "I know that I would be better for this company than

The Blame Game

Mr. Franklin"—so the story that you are telling about him (which may be true), may not be *that* dishonest. You can convince yourself that this blame serves a greater good.

A Deceitful Blame in your business may occur when you are knowingly selling an inferior or inexpensive brand or model of a product to save money; or nefariously selling it as a superior product (for a superior price). You know that many people may be dissatisfied with what you are selling but you decide to go ahead anyway. You reason that once your business becomes more successful, you will no longer have to buy the cheapest brand products on the market and you can get your customers better goods and services.

As expected, you get a few customers returning the items. You act surprised when this happens and shift the responsibility and blame to the manufacturer. You say that this is the last time you will do business with that manufacturer, how dare they send an inferior product. After all, you, the customer, are his primary concern.

6. Who We Blame

"We are taught you must blame your father, your sisters, your brothers, the school, the teachers—you can blame anyone, but never blame yourself. It's never your fault, because if you want to change, you're the one who has got to change. It's as simple as that, isn't it?"

Katherine Hepburn

The list of who we blame is quite extensive and I don't want to be blamed for leaving anyone off the list. Last and least, we blame ourselves. Many of us do not partake in this style of blaming very often. This is typically not our first choice of who to blame, yet there are times when it is certainly to our advantage to blame ourselves. For any wrongdoing, mistakes, or what we believe to be intentional misappropriations, we often accuse those close to us—family members, friends, and spouses. At work, we blame bosses and co-workers; concomitantly bosses blame employees for mistakes and lack of production. It doesn't matter what level of education you are in, from preschool until college, everybody is to blame. Teachers blame students and students blame teachers. It's been like this since antiquity. The easiest category is people whom we don't know.

Ourselves

There is a fine line between accepting responsibility at times that we should indeed be accountable (a good thing), and blaming ourselves whether or not we are liable (a bad thing). Most people shy away from being accountable. They are quick to perform a responsibility shift the moment that accusing eyes start turning toward them. When good people do something that they know is wrong, they try to explain their behavior by externalizing—attributing the cause and blame to something other than themselves.

Why then would we ever blame ourselves for anything if it's so easy and acceptable to blame others? There's an old adage that with age comes wisdom. But sometimes age just comes alone. Well, with every externalization comes blame. Every time that I attribute my bad behavior to something outside myself, I am creating a blaming environment. But, sometimes blame just comes alone. When we don't externalize and blame others, we often turn the blaming finger at ourselves. This typically occurs when we truly are not liable or responsible in any way for bad things that have happened. Rabbi Harold Kushner addresses this point: "We are so guilt-prone, unable to accept the fact that there may be lots of reasons for something not working out, because at some perverse level, it feels good to feel bad. To assume the blame is to make ourselves feel important, indispensable." It is interesting that the process of externalization and the process of self-blame both cater to our fantasies of grandiosity.

When something horrible happens that is beyond my understanding or beyond my control, then I will take the blame. It is as if I am suggesting that I can change the course of nature, create action at a distance, or alter the behavior of others. We blame ourselves for things with which no one would ever associate or accuse us. I could not be responsible for the huge rainfall that ruined the family picnic, but I can act like a martyr and take the blame. "It rained because I have been complaining for the past few days about how dry my grass is and how badly we need the rain. I've been praying for rain and now here it is. I'll take the blame on this one." Remember, whenever you point your index finger at someone or something in an effort to show blame, you are simultaneously pointing four other fingers back toward yourself in a subtle self-blame.

As Oscar Wilde has stated, "There is luxury in self reproach. When we blame ourselves, we feel no one else has a right to blame us." When we put ourselves down for certain behaviors or mistakes, we believe that we take away this opportunity for others to treat us harshly. If I'm the first to blame me and I do so in a self-deprecating fashion, maybe everyone else will change their feelings from frustration and anger to empathy and compassion. They'll see what I'm going through and feel sorry for me, not blame me!

Family

Parents blame their children and children blame their siblings. In time, children also blame their parents and grandparents. Sibling blame is a behavior that accompanies many people throughout their lives. Even as adults, we blame siblings for our disappointments and hardships. Sources of blame may include our living situation, current job positions, perceived parental favoritism, or anything that doesn't go completely smoothly at a family function. How many families do you know or have heard of where siblings haven't spoken to each other for several years? In many cases neither one even remembers the initial cause of the severed relationship.

Fortunately, the Blame Game, Anniversary Family Edition, does not limit itself to siblings; everyone may participate. Our family members have known us longer than any of our other relationships. This increases the comfort level that we have with our siblings and other family members even when we are mad at them or not communicating with them. We hope for unconditional love and so we set the bar high. We accuse and blame our siblings, our parents, and our children knowing that we are the only family that they have. It is hard (but not impossible) to disown a relative. How often do we hear young children complaining to their parents, "I didn't get to go and it's all your fault"? As with sibling blame the pattern of parental blame is often carried into adulthood. As comedienne Joan Rivers stated, "I blame my mother for my poor sex life. All she told me was, 'The man goes on top and the woman underneath.' For three years my husband and I slept in bunk beds." An anonymous author on the blog TherapyIsExpensive.net wrote, "Youth is when you blame all your troubles on your parents; maturity is when you learn that everything is the fault of the younger generation."

In the end it feels good to have a reason for your failures; an excuse for why you are in a bad marriage, living in a bad neighborhood, why you have no friends, why your children don't respect you, and why you are stuck in a low-paying, low-prestige, unsatisfying job. Obviously, parental blame is not limited to social situations. You can also blame your parents for your genetic makeup. "I was great in basketball; I could have been an NBA all-star... if I was just two feet taller. It's my parents fault, they're both short." We can get a lot of mileage out of this type of blaming and it really does a great job excusing us from not achieving any level of success or self-satisfaction.

Familial Blame is excellent when used inter-generationally. I have premature gray hair and balding. Big decision to make... do I blame my parents and maladaptive genetics or do I blame my kids for stressing me out? Personally, I take a third option. I'll blame the male hormone testosterone. An increase in testosterone is associated with baldness. I must be a manly man to be losing my hair at this age.

Blaming family members is an interesting phenomenon. This behavior would be unacceptable if delivered to our friends, acquaintances, or business associates. Yet it becomes very natural and sadly well-accepted to direct this mind-set toward our siblings and even parents.

Friends

What are friends for if not for blaming? Each year we come up with new and exciting ways to blame our friends. Starting as young children we transfer some of our sibling blame to accusing our buddies. We waste no time explaining to our parents that, "Jimmy made me do it" or "all my friends were doing it, so I thought it would be okay." When we blame friends, it is best that they aren't around to hear it and that the blame doesn't get back to them; unless of course you really want to check the solidity of your friendship. In general, blaming friends takes the form of an Innocent, Subtle, or Casual Blame.

Occasionally we're lucky enough to be able to blame friends for our inadequacies, failures, or bad behavior. But how about blaming friends for our physical features? You might think this is stretching the limits of our blamability. The Framingham Study is an ongoing, long-term data collection that began in 1948 to investigate heart disease and its risk factors. In 2002, published data from the study showed that excess body weight is strongly associated with an increased risk of heart failure. In 2007, the researchers published data in the *New England Journal of Medicine*, which was discussed in the *New York Times* article "Find Yourself Packing It On? Blame Friends," by Gina Kolata. If an individual has an overweight friend, then he or she is more likely to gain weight. When one person in a social network gains weight, his or her friends are also likely to gain weight. If a close friend gained weight, an individual had a 57 percent chance of gaining weight. Neighbors and family members had almost no effect on an individual's chance of gaining weight.

This may be the beginning of some wonderful blames that we haven't even begun to tap into. Think of all the bad habits that our friends exhibit that we can adopt as our own, and blame them for our actions. Smoking, drug use, drinking, and poor social behaviors are all possible. While these are not new blames, we have not previously had the scientific backing of the *New England Journal of Medicine* to solidify our lack of responsibility.

Spouses

Spouses are one of the most convenient sources of Casual or Innocent Blames. Even those involved in loving, productive relationships will still take advantage of their spouses by focusing the blame. Who else is better to attribute my sleeping in past my alarm, staying up late, waking in the middle of the night, not having clean clothes to wear, the car being dented, the roof leaking, our uncontrollable kids—the list can go on forever. The purpose of these blames is not meant to cause harm. Since our spouses are often adept at picking up our subtle signs of negativity, we want to make sure that these blames, when delivered, are not associated with negative motivations, thoughts, or emotions that may adversely affect our relationships. This is a blame of convenience, not malice.

In the midst of poor relationships, even prior to legal actions being sought, such as separation or divorce, the spousal blames transition from Casual and Innocent to Blatant, Subtle, and Secret, and finally to the Big D. These types of blames are to position us for improved custody or financial battles. They also help us distribute our ill feelings toward our future ex-spouses without actually having to purchase large-font ads in the local newspaper. They are reaffirmations for our feelings of repression, suppression, depression, and oppression caused, of course, by our spouses.

During my first marriage, I grew unhappy with my job; too much stress, not enough family time. I wanted to start a new career in something else, anything else. For several years I had discussions with my wife about trying to cut down hours at the hospital and start a new line of work. I had several ideas including: real estate, teaching martial arts, and writing books. She was more practical than I was and pointed out that we would have to completely change our lifestyle and couldn't afford to have me do this. I blamed her for my unhappiness, rather than take responsibility for my lack of action. In reality, I was not ready to make a move, feared changing horses in the middle of the stream, and blamed her for my lack of courage and indecision. However, the responsibility for change rested solely in my hands.

Bosses and co-workers

There are three main varieties of Blaming at the office that we'll discuss. The first is Boss Blaming, the second is Co-worker Blaming, and finally Employee Blaming.

The 1961 Robert Morse film *How to Succeed in Business Without Really Trying* reflected the underlying belief that one should be able to enjoy reasonable success in business without too much effort. We see other people with less aptitude achieve success at similar, and at times simpler, jobs. So, why aren't we financially independent, enormously wealthy, free from significant job stress, and going to work with complete career satisfaction? Obviously, you are not attaining your peak potential in your current profession because you are being psychologically held back by your boss. Your boss is the one that determines your salary, bonus, job description, vacation time, job location, level of involvement with the company, potential for advancement, and perhaps your overall financial success. If you are not content with your current position, who else are you going to blame?

Your boss doesn't understand you or your needs, and just as importantly, she doesn't fully appreciate the needs of the company or how to make things happen. Or alternatively, your boss probably slept his way to the top or inherited the company from a rich grandfather. All great reasons to blame. Our coworkers are frequently a great source of moral support when it comes to blaming the supervisor because there is the common goal of "success" and the common complaint of being unsuccessful. Misery loves company. Unfortunately, you may feel that misery loves your company more than others.

Many of us feel free to blame and criticize higher-level management for not doing things our way. We often rely on, in fact we depend on, our co-workers for backing us up when Boss Blaming. Otherwise, what would be the use of those heated discussions around the water cooler? This is a great example of a Group Blame. All persons in supervisor positions and management positions are free game. There is power in numbers and recruiting coworkers who are also dissatisfied with their situation and are looking for similar blaming rights is an easy way to increase your authority. Let's remember those famous words, "United we stand, divided we fall."

Let's focus on the second half of that insightful saying, "divided we fall." Yes, we're going to refocus our efforts on blaming some of those co-workers with whom you have just bonded. The second type of office blame is to accuse your co-workers. After all, not everyone can get promoted at the same time. We can't all be managers and supervisors. The company may have limited resources and limited finances; therefore, the larger your bonus and the greater your raise, the smaller my bonus and my raise. Even in the rare cases of unlimited resources, the promotion to middle management and supervisory positions are often highly competitive. This is every person for themselves. When it comes to blaming co-workers try to focus on Casual, Subtle, Secret Blames.

Of course, there is always the "Big D," Deceitful Blames, for those who are really motivated to succeed and are willing to take the higher risks involved. Blatant Blames should be held to a minimum in an open workplace.

The third type of blame in the office environment involves the blame rolling downhill phenomenon; the boss blames the employee. Just as employees complain about their job situation but many would not change it for an upper level management position if given the opportunity, management also complain about their job situation but would not trade it to move down the corporate ladder. So, how do they stay where they are? When the business is doing well, it is important that everyone realize how vitally important that manager or supervisor is to the corporation. It is critical that we understand how responsible that manager is and what a key player he or she is to any and all successes that the business enjoys. It is also very critical that everyone understand that when bad things happen in the business, it is typically because of some employee who has not complied with that supervisor. You must understand that this is the one thing for which the supervisor is not responsible. They must engage in some Blatant (and at times Deceitful) Blames to maintain their job security. They must do what is necessary to shift responsibility downhill. It is never a good thing to be the target of these types of accusations.

Teachers and students

Similar in form to boss and employee relationships are the teacher and student associations. One of the more commonplace blames is the student blaming the teacher. The parents initiate this type of blame and help teach it to their children from a very young age. Our children overhear us complaining about their teachers whenever our children aren't doing well in school. They are our offspring, and as such they are all geniuses. Therefore, if they are not doing well in school or not able to grasp a concept, it stands to reason that this is a teacher problem, not a student problem. Not only does it not have anything to do with the fact that Johnny isn't paying attention in class or listening to the assignments, but if he had a better teacher, she would be able to command better awareness and concentration. This is not just true for kindergarten and grade schoolers; we continue this pattern throughout high school, college, trade school, graduate school, medical school, medical residencies, and any other location that teachers may be found.

No teacher is immune. I don't do well in a Taekwondo tournament; it had nothing to do with not listening to my coach. It is simply because my teacher was not as good as some of the other teachers. He didn't prepare me well enough. Oh sure, I got so nervous that I forgot everything. But if he were a better teacher, I wouldn't have been so nervous. I would have been much more confident. Every bad test result can, in some way or another, ultimately be blamed on a teacher. Of course, using this reasoning we must put on blinders and at least pretend to be ignorant to those individuals who did quite well on the quiz or exam. In these cases, we try to reason that they are either freakishly gifted or must have learned the material from another source. Some bad results don't prove a teacher is bad. Likewise, some good results can't prove a teacher is good. We have the ability to learn the material because of a good teacher or despite a bad teacher.

What goes around comes around. As the students accuse the teachers for their poor performance, the teachers are also on the attack, blaming the students for the results. Bad grades and poor performance don't look very good on a teacher's record. Why are the students having such a hard time learning this material? The answer seems pretty obvious: I've got a really bad bunch of students. Or, I've got a few rowdy students who are making it difficult for the others to get a lot out of the lessons. In either case, it has nothing to do with my ability to teach the material. I have a firm grasp on the subject matter and understand the best way to convey this information.

The teacher may view the students as having a receptive aphasia: a disorder involving an inability to pick up or learn new information. While the students view the teacher as having an expressive aphasia: a hard time explaining what she means. This may be referred to as a Brain Blame.

Dr. I.M. Right is a surgeon; an excellent technician in terms of his surgical skills but a less-than-skilled communicator when it comes to dealing with coworkers. One day he has a case scheduled for 9:00 a.m. to follow after another surgeon. The previous case finishes early and the nurses and anesthesiologist page Dr. Right several times to see if he can get there early, but get no response. A physician assistant says that Dr. Right is in the hospital and we can go ahead with his patient. After a few more pages to Dr. Right and ninety minutes later, they call Dr. Right's secretary who says that Dr. Right was not at work. Shortly afterward, Dr. Right walks into the hallway from the surgeon's lounge and states in an accusing tone, "So, are we going to get this case started or not?" It's pointed out to Dr. Right that they had been paging him for an hour and a half. Dr. Right replies, "That's not true. I never got a single page!"

He then looks down and finds that he is missing his pager, "Oh, it looks like my beeper disappeared." He is told that they had called his office, paged overhead, and have been waiting for a long time. He then goes on to an award winning blame-shift, explaining, "My secretary never knows what's going on. You shouldn't have asked her. I don't usually schedule cases for Monday mornings but I had an opening so the surgery scheduling nurse told me I could start at 10:00 a.m.

She changed the time and didn't tell me. I went to a conference at 8:00 a.m. and the person running the conference started late and went over his allotted time. My beeper must have slipped off my scrubs this morning—these are lousy scrubs and those new pagers never seem to stay on. I've been sitting in the lounge for the past hour waiting for *you*. There were so many people in the lounge talking that it's impossible to hear any overhead pages in there. You and the nurse and my physician assistant should know that I would be sitting in the lounge waiting for you if I have a case to do. You should have just walked in there and found me. Besides this family is so unreliable, I didn't think that they were actually going to show up to have the surgery done."

Dr. Right is so good at creating and presenting this chain-of-blame that the rest of the team is now ready to apologize. He is completely oblivious to his own role in taking care of his eight-year- old patient. The IBF was notified and Dr. Right received a Master-Blamer certificate and a nomination for the Blaming Hall of Fame.

Strangers

American playwright Tennessee Williams is famous for his quote, "I have always depended on the kindness of strangers." I teach my children that being kind to strangers is a wonderful thing. I still believe in the concept of "stranger danger"; however, everyone has value and we should be slow to judge. When we are kind to strangers, we expand our horizons and become better people. This is the ideal, but what is the real deal? The reality is that strangers make easy blaming targets. It is hard for strangers to defend themselves from these accusations-at-a-distance. We don't have to concern ourselves with repercussions and we hope to not have reason to get to know these people at a later date. The more distant the associations between the blamee and the blamer, the more trouble-free the blame.

Strangers do not get the benefit of the doubt that we occasionally and sparingly might be willing to give to our close friends and sometimes family. We do this for two reasons. First, strangers have not earned this privilege. Second, we would lose out on some great blaming opportunities. It is peculiar that when strangers perform acts of kindness or exhibit positive behaviors, we tend to view these activities as being situationally-determined. They were forced into acting in a constructive way by the situation, not because of their innate goodness.

We encounter Stranger Blame multiple times every day. When someone makes an unexpected turn in front of you; gets in front of you in line at the movie theater; gets into a car accident a mile ahead of you on the freeway and there is a gawking delay as drivers slow down to examine the accident; has too many groceries at the checkout line – each one of them deserves to be blamed for you being late for work.

Another form of Stranger Blame that we frequently witness is that of Group Blaming. In his book, *From Da to Yes: Understanding the East Europeans,* Yale Richmond describes the well-known practice of Eastern European Blaming. Slovaks blame Czechs, Romanians and Hungarians blame each other, Ukrainians and Poles blame Russians, Lithuanians blame Poles, Croats and Serbs blame each other, Muslim Serbs blame Christian Serbs, all Eastern Europeans blame the Soviets, and "whatever blame is left over is heaped upon Gypsies and Jews."

Eastern Europe does not have a patent on Stranger Blame. Hate groups, such as Neo-Nazis, exist around the world to disseminate and advocate violence toward members of a specific race, ethnicity, religion, sexual orientation, gender, or other specific sector of society. These organizations of hate energize their members by blaming their victims for the ills of society and making them into scapegoats.

Every country in the world encourages Group Blaming of strangers. A fine cinematic example of this is a 1995 film produced and directed by Michael Moore, *Canadian Bacon*. In this movie, a U.S. president (played by Alan Alda), initiates a war with Canada to distract voters from domestic troubles and revitalize the economy. To invigorate the citizens, the publicity campaign blames Canadians for American problems. John Candy as Sheriff Bud B. Boomer, takes the offensive American position and the Canadians are warned by the threat, "You surrender pronto, or we'll level Toronto." As a Canadian citizen and former Torontonian, I was a little put out. I'll blame Michael Moore!

7. What We Blame

"I never blame myself when I'm not hitting. I just blame the bat, and if it keeps up, I change bats. After all, if I know it isn't my fault that I'm not hitting, how can I get mad at myself?"

Yogi Berra

Included in "what" to blame are some favorite targets including: God, nature, genetics, animals, miscellaneous items such as cars, cameras and mechanical devices, items used to help us physically like glasses, and our very own bodies. While the government may also be included in the "what" category, it is such an important topic that it deserved it's own section – chapter 8.

You will not only be familiar with all of the categories, but you will undoubtedly have spent time blaming all or most of the things listed. This is not a complete inventory of potential blaming targets; far from it. This is merely a list and brief description of some of the more popular targets of blame. What else is fair game to blame? Everything! For example, comedian Allan Carr quipped, "A lot of comedians, when they have a bad gig, will blame everything but themselves. They'll blame the crowd, or the room was wrong, it had a weird vibe, or the promoter promoted a weird atmosphere." If I've left off some of your favorite blame aims, please don't hesitate to blame me.

God

"If you don't do your part, don't blame God," exclaimed Billy Sunday, an influential athlete and religious figure in the first two decades of the twentieth century. An old Indian proverb states, "Do not blame God for having created the tiger, but thank him for not having given it wings." It would be relatively easy to spend the rest of this book on the subject of God and what is or isn't under the control of the almighty. Rabbi David Cooper spent an entire book discussing why I should not have even put this topic in the "What Do We Blame" chapter, since he argues very convincingly that "God is a Verb" not a noun. While I agree with Rabbi Cooper, I didn't have room for a chapter titled "Verbs That We Blame," so bear with me. I will take the blame for this.

As the comedian Henny Youngman said, "I once wanted to become an atheist, but I gave up—they have no holidays." The funny thing about accusing God for bad things that happen to us is that even some atheists blame God for the state of the world. "Thank God I don't have to do any Christmas shopping." Whether it is the Judeo-Christian God of the Old Testament, Allah of the Koran, Jesus of the New Testament, Buddha, or any number of Hindu, Native American, or African Gods or God-like deities, there are many who believe in something, someone, or some verb-like force that is greater than us. Rabbi David Aaron writes in his book *Seeing God* that he was told by someone of their disbelief in God. Rabbi Aaron replies, "I don't believe in the same God that you don't believe in." All theists have their personal version of what God is to them.

For purposes of simplicity, I'm going to call most of it God. In no way does this mean to imply that my God is better than your God. If that was indeed the case, your God might blame my God (OMG). The important thing that is consistent is our ability to personally blame whichever God or energy life source that we believe to exist. Many people believe that God has ultimate control—the ultimate responsibility for our thoughts, feelings, and actions. We, as a society, have blamed God since Adam first interacted with God in the Original Blame and we have continued to do so since that time. One of the best advantages of a belief in God is the promise that you can also blame God when things don't go your way. It should be logical that the more responsibility that you place in God's hands, the more you should be able to blame God for bad stuff that transpires. However, even those who don't believe in God still hold him responsible for their ill fate — "an act of God." Whereas those that are the strongest believers in God may tend to place less blame on him. While many atheists use the "Why do bad things happen?" question to try to support their view of a godless world, others may reason that bad things occurring legitimizes the blaming of God.

Many people believe in a personal Judeo-Christian God with whom you can bargain; "If you let me pass this exam, I'll go to church every Sunday," or "If you make me not be late for this interview, I won't procrastinate anymore," or "If you get me the winning lottery ticket, I promise to give the money to charity." If God is truly responsible for allowing or causing all these events to happen, then obviously we are fully justified in blaming God for pretty much anything that we perceive as negative that happens to us.

To some, God may control all facets of our lives and micromanage all of our daily affairs. We ask that he help us get to work safely, pass exams, not allow it to rain during our office picnic, run faster to win my race, get me great cards for my next hand in poker, etc. If God is omnipotent, then he has the ability to control everything, for the good or the bad. Thus, bad things happen because God made them happen. We are either being punished, taught a lesson, being tested, our faith is being strengthened, or the reason simply is far beyond our understanding. Who are we to judge or question or even hope to understand God's plan for us and for the universe? While this philosophy may make the world more organized and understandable, these answers typically add a burden to the one suffering, rather than relieving their stress. This view of the world also takes away any perceived control over our own lives and removes all of our responsibility for our own fate. In this frame of mind, we must learn to accept whatever happens to us. This theory guides us to believe that no matter how bad things seem, what some would interpret as happening *to* us, we'll think of it as happening *for* us, or for the greater good. For those who truly share this belief system, that God is a micromanager, it is difficult to blame God for anything.

In the book of Samuel, we read about King David and the sins that he committed. He sleeps with Bathsheba, the wife of Uriah. When Bathsheba becomes pregnant, King David sends Uriah back into battle and gives instructions to the commander, Joab, to abandon Uriah on the battlefield so that he may be murdered. David then marries Bathsheba and they have a son. But King David's actions displeased the Lord... So God then punishes him by giving his wives (he had many) to other men and killing his son. So with this lesson in mind, it may not seem unreasonable to blame God for horrific events that we don't understand. Was this the best way to punish David— by killing an innocent child? How about the wives? Was it his punishment or theirs that they were sent around to other men?

Many of us can't imagine the horror of our family being destroyed by a hurricane, our parents dying in a car crash, or a child being kidnapped and murdered. To be completely accepting of all of it, even thanking God for his unquestioned wisdom without blaming, is extremely difficult. It would be easier to accept the notion that a horrible event occurring is a punishment if there were some type of obvious connection or association between the two. For example, one must have a terrific imagination to justify the death of an innocent infant as punishment for sins that their mother or father committed. There are no lessons for the infant to have learned, and the death of an infant seems like an extreme way of enhancing a parents' faith in God. Did God do this to help parents push toward more safety standards or donate more money for infant research? Possible, but still too high a price for me.

Similar questions were asked by Elie Wiesel, who in his book *Night* provides a true, first-person account of his experiences as a young boy in the Nazi death camps of World War II. Experiencing the brutality of the concentration camps, he loses his faith in God and wonders how God could make this happen. He states, "I did not deny God's existence, but I doubted His absolute justice." These feelings are also verbalized in the 2003 movie *Bruce Almighty*. Bruce Nolan, a TV news reporter played by Jim Carry, blames God for everything that's going wrong with his life. He explains to his girlfriend how God is an angry kid with a magnifying glass, and Bruce is the ant. Bruce complains to God that he is doing a poor job as supreme deity. God, played by Morgan Freeman, then grants Bruce supreme power to see if he can do a better job. Bruce uses his new-found powers to sabotage the colleague that screwed him over so that he can get a better job, transform his car from a Datson to a Saleen S7 supercar, allow his favorite hockey team to get over a slump, go to the Stanley Cup playoffs, and enhance his girlfriend's breasts and sex drive. After being reminded that he also has to take care of other people's problems, he tries to answer prayers by giving everyone everything they want, resulting in world riots and mayhem. So Bruce gives up on being God and gets on his knees begging God to let him be himself once again.

Underlying this belief system is a deep and unrelenting anger at God and a refusal to be responsible for one's own situation. If God is always around, then God is always convenient to blame. While blaming Hitler or the Nazis in general was certainly appropriate, it did little to heal the heart or soul, or save the lives of the victims.

A popular belief is the contention that God set up the milieu; he got the ball rolling and has given us free will to make our own decisions. Bad things that happen do so because God has not *caused* them to happen but has *allowed* them to happen. Rabbi Harold Kushner is a foremost religious authority and author of the bestselling book *Why Bad Things Happen to Good People*. If God has given us free will, then bad events that are inflicted by evil individuals are due to bad decisions and bad people. If God were to selectively stop specific events and people, the loss of our free will would be an even greater problem for the world. In one scene of the movie *Bruce Almighty*, Bruce asks God, "How do you make someone love you without affecting their free will?" God responds, "Heh, welcome to my world, son. If you come up with an answer to that one, you let me know." If God is the one who gave us free will in the first place and could have stopped horrors such as the Holocaust but chose not to, he should bear the blame. Yes, we also can place some of the blame on the perpetrators who committed the acts.

It may sometimes be difficult to determine what events are "God-ordained." Barbaric military missions that involve glaring human rights abuses in direct opposition to the messages from God are supported by clergy, supposedly in the name of God. Omari Jackson, in his online article (http://www.theperspective.org/Blaming.html). "Blaming God For Our Actions," has written about a cleric who attributed seven years of social disorder and over 300,000 Liberians murdered to an act of God. He also quotes Mr. Louis Farrakhan of the Nation of Islam as saying that God used the seven years to bring Liberians back to Him. "The blood of all those murdered, massacred, and butchered," Farrakhan said, "would purify the Liberian nation." As these events have been erroneously attributed to God, does that not allow us to blame Him for their occurrence?

In 2006, Tornados tore through Tennessee, destroyed hundreds of homes and killed at least thirty-four people. Tennessee Governor Phil Bredesen was quoted by the *Associated Press* as stating, "It looks like the Lord took a Brillo pad and scrubbed the ground." When referring to thunderstorm and tornado damage, Governor Bredesen stated, "The wrath of God is the only way I can describe it." The Online Nashville News article entitled, "God Prefers SOS Pads" (http://www.nashvillescene.com), has quoted a retort from Bill Hobbs' February 8, 2008, blog Stop Blaming God. "He [God] is in the outpouring of help for the victims that got underway before the last raindrops fell and the last of the winds died down. He is in the comfort and support the families who lost people are receiving from family, friends, and neighbors... And He is in the brilliance and creativity of the people who created technologies that gave people advance warning of the storms, so that many hundreds more weren't killed. He wasn't in the tornados." I guess this would remove much of the God blame.

An "act of God" is a legal term for events outside of human control, such as sudden floods or other natural disasters, for which no person can be held responsible. In contract law, in an act of God the promise is discharged because of unforeseen, naturally occurring events that were unavoidable and which would result in insurmountable delay, expense, or other material breach. Under the Uniform Commercial Code, failure to deliver goods sold may be excused by an act of God if the absence of such act was a "basic assumption" of the contract, but has made the delivery commercially "impracticable."

In tort law, an act of God may be a type of intervening cause, the lack of which would have avoided the cause or decreased the result of liability. For example, even an old, poorly constructed building would still be standing if not for the earthquake. However, foreseeable results of unforeseeable causes may still raise liability. For example, a ship owner may be solely responsible or perhaps *share* liability with God if he didn't take reasonable precautions to protect his ship carrying volatile compressed gas against sparks and lightning strikes. In 1915, the city of San Diego hired Charles Hatfield for $10,000 to fill the Morena reservoir to capacity with rainwater. The region was soon flooded by heavy rains, nearly bursting the reservoir's dam, killing nearly twenty people, destroying over one hundred bridges, knocking out telephone and telegraph lines, and causing an estimated $3.5 million in total damages. When the city refused to pay him (he had forgotten to sign the contract), he sued the city. The floods were ruled an act of God, excluding him from both liability and from payment. Should it come as any surprise in this day and age that not only can we turn to a court of law for a determination as to what is actually an act of God but we can rely on the legal system to determine if God is to blame!

Another example of legally blaming God was the multimillion-dollar class action lawsuit against Bayer for contamination of U.S. rice crops with unapproved genetically engineered rice called LL601. In court documents, Bayer claimed the contamination was due to acts of God or the rice farmers themselves. Blaming the farmers was not a surprise since it was the farmers who were suing Bayer for lost income. Shifting responsibility to God was certainly a great precedent for big business bouncing blames.

Satan

I know that many of you will suggest that I should have included this in the "Who" chapter, yet there will be some that will say that I should have included this in the previous section on God. For centuries, a great target of blame is Satan. John 8:44 states, "It is the life's work of the devil and his demons to cause as much human suffering as possible." The New Testament refers to Satan as always working, suggesting, and conniving. Any bad thing that happens to anyone may be attributed, at least in part, to persuasion by the devil. This useful fall back can be applied in many ways, be they natural disasters or human-inflicted events. When someone acts badly, they are said to possess the devil. "They have the devil in them." "They were taken over by Satan." As we witnessed in the movie *The Exorcist*, head-spinning, foul language, disrupting parents, and generally horrific behavior may be blamed on Satan.

My favorite responsibility shift blaming Satan, "The devil made me do it." This phrase is useful in almost every situation where you intentionally or unintentionally caused harm or dismay. Use it for anything that you said or did that you should not have; or anything that you didn't say or didn't do that you should have. This blame is typically reserved for small-ticket items, al- though it certainly may be incorporated into a legal defense when pleading insanity.

Nature

Whether you believe nature to be a thinking and rational force or simply an enormously impressive noun with an attitude, it may certainly be blamed for many things, foremost of which are natural disasters and catastrophes. Michael Novak, author, philosopher, and theologian, wrote an article published by the

National Review Online in 2005 titled, *"Blaming God First: Why do children have to die?"* Blaming God was not his suggestion but his analysis of what nihilists and atheists have done to explain "natural disasters" such as the tsunami in Indonesia in December, 2004 that took the lives of at least 230,000 people in eleven countries. The Tsunami was an Indian Ocean earthquake with waves up to one hundred feet. It was one of the deadliest natural disasters in history. He explains that some atheists are rationalists, believing that in the end, there is order, purpose, and rational laws directing the course of the universe. However, they don't feel comfortable with naming this system God. Other atheists are nihilists who believe that there are no governing laws or order; no underlying system or reason for anything. Nowak explains how there is no reason of course for atheists to invoke God; except at times of "natural disasters" when they bring up the question, *How could a Judeo-Christian God do this?* Yes, in the end, even many atheists blame God. There may be a feeling of intellectual superiority derived from denying the existence of God and the uselessness of religion. However, there are also feelings of purpose, retribution, and resolve when there is a target of blame.

I was in an operating room at Stanford Hospital on October 17, 1989, when the room started to move. This 7.1 earthquake that struck the Bay Area just before the third game of the World Series at Candlestick Park was the worst earthquake since 1906. There were sixty-two deaths, over 3,700 injuries, and more than 12,000 left homeless. There was six billion dollars in damage including: collapse of part of the San Francisco-Oakland Bay Bridge, power outages, loss of emergency telephone service, multiple fires, partial destruction of Interstate 280, and a four-foot tsunami in Monterey Bay. There was plenty of devastation and blamage to be placed on that earthquake.

Several years ago I was on a medical mission in the town of Bucaramanga, Columbia. I was providing anesthesia for a pediatric patient when the surgeon quickly grew angry with me and blamed me for not doing an adequate job: "Neil, can't you give something to stop him from moving." I was just about to apologize for not providing enough anesthesia when I realized that not only was the patient moving, but everything was moving. We were at the beginning of an earthquake! Well thank God, I could blame Mother Nature. I could have written this same story in the section on God. I could have written, Well thank Mother Nature, I could blame God. Natural disasters are not limited to earthquakes and tsunamis.

Other known natural disasters include tornados, volcanoes, hurricanes, floods, limnic eruptions, landslides, avalanches, lahars (a type of mudflow), thunderstorms, snowstorms, sandstorms, hail- storms, drought, heat waves, cyclones, fires, blizzards, famine, lightning, some diseases and epidemics, events involving space products such as meteorites and solar flares.

We should appreciate that the term "natural disaster" is related to the presence of humans or at least some form of animal life. For example, few people would classify solar flares as a natural disaster. However, the amount of energy released from a solar flare is equivalent to millions of 100-megaton hydrogen bombs and about ten million times greater than the energy released from an active volcano. But since people are not physically compromised during solar flares (unless you stare at them), they are referred to fondly as beautiful, natural phenomena. As such, natural disasters, which have the capacity to cause injury, are typically associated with blame. It is like the old Zen question, "If a man talks in the forest and no one is around to hear him, is he still wrong?" Or perhaps, if a tree falls in the forest and no one is around, 1) Does it make a sound? and 2) Who do we blame? The answer is that if an immense force of nature occurs and no one is around to be involved in it or hurt by it, we call it a natural hazard or simply nature. We don't add the term disaster until there is *devastation* that may involve blame.

There are whole books devoted to blaming specific facets of nature. *Blame it on the Weather* by David Phillips, Suzanne Chisholm, and Michael Parfit, and *Blame It on the Rain: How the Weather Has Changed History* by Laura Lee. But it doesn't stop there. You don't have to limit yourself to blaming everything under the sun, since you can even find the book *Blame it on the Sun*.

In addition to blaming nature for devastating events occurring in our lives, we are all aware that nature may be blamed for other things—like mood swings causing us to act in certain ways. The common phrase, "It's only natural" typically implies that something occurred naturally (i.e., without help or intervention). However, there may be a deeper meaning to this simple phrase when used by philosophical naturalists. Modern naturalism has a basis in rationalism and science. All phenomena have natural explanations. Thus, stating "It's only natural" allows us to blame nature, minimize the importance or implications of the events and remove our responsibility for our actions.

Cynthia was caught in traffic and needed to get home to cook dinner for her family. She made a quick stop at the grocery store to pick up a few items for that night. The checkout lines were long and she was in a hurry, so she maneuvered her way in front of an elderly man who was just about to go through the checkout with a large shopping cart full of food. "It's only natural that I went ahead of him, he would have taken so long that I wouldn't have ever made it home from work to get dinner for the kids." I can cut someone off in line, not return incorrect change, sneak into an early showing of a movie when no one is watching, etc. For each of these "minor" infractions, I can rather quietly and innocently exclaim, "It's only natural." In other words, "Don't blame me." In this sense, "It's only natural" may refer to Darwinian theory of survival of the fittest. If I do things for my personal benefit over the concern of others, and claim that this is natural and thus acceptable, perhaps it will lead to a greater chance of me prospering (or propagating?).

Genetics

Obesity: We have discussed how to successfully blame your friends for your obesity problem. But if you decide that you would rather not involve other people, you can always blame genetics. A genetic variant, near the fat metabolism gene, predisposing people to obesity was identified by researchers at Boston University. Although several obesity-related genes are already known, they affect specific families and are rare in the general population. The genetic variant found in 2006 (*Science*, Volume 312) is common, occurring in 10 percent of the populations studied. The link is between obesity and a short section of the genome that lies between two genes. Because the variant is found in African populations, it probably arose before modern humans left Africa (50,000 years ago). The genome was most likely harmless until modern times, when some new aspect of the human environment (high-calorie food would be appropriate to blame) interacted with it to raise the risk of obesity. "Those who inherit two copies of the variant, one from each parent, have a 22 percent extra risk of becoming obese," says Dr. Herbert, a member of the research team.

If your parents are overweight and have passed on poor eating habits, you can either continue to indulge in those self-defeating manners or choose to change your lifestyle and take care of your problem. Alternatively, you can assume that you were blessed with a genetically-predisposed reason, blame genetics and have a great excuse for your diagnosis. You can give weight loss a half-hearted attempt, but all future failures can be easily blamed on your faulty genome.

Smoking: Quitting smoking is extremely difficult for some; only 20 percent actually succeed in quitting. The reason was previously believed to be a physical addiction to nicotine and a psychological addiction to smoking. However, research has now found that a certain gene can make the difference as to whether or not someone has a greater likelihood of starting to smoke, becoming nicotine addicted, and possibly getting lung cancer. MSNBC online (http://www.msnbc.msn.com/id/23919596) has referred to the results of these studies (published in *Nature* and *NatureGenetics*, 2008) as, "Can't quit smoking? Blame your genes." People carrying a particular version of the dopamine transporter gene are less likely to start smoking before age sixteen and are more likely to quit smoking if they start. People with this particular genotype are those with a lower novelty-seeking trait, which correlated with less desire to smoke. Thus, it seems very reasonable that if you are trying to quit smoking and having a rather difficult time doing so, you can probably assume that you were not lucky enough to be born with this "quitting genome."

Height: Height generally varies little between people. Exceptional height variation is usually due to gigantism or dwarfism. At 8 feet, 5.5 inches, Leonid Stadnyk from Ukraine is the world's tallest living man. Height is, like other phenotypic traits, determined by a combination of genetics and environmental factors, such as nutrition. Genetically speaking, the heights of mother and son and of father and daughter correlate, suggesting that a short mother will more likely bear a shorter son, and tall fathers will have tall daughters. There is an accumulative generation effect such that nutrition and health over generations influences the height of descendants to varying degrees. Your mother's health prior to and during pregnancy has a role in determining your height.

Human height is 90 percent heritable and is considered polygenic or multifactorial. The only gene so far attributed with normal height variation is HMGA2. This is only one of many, as each copy of the allele concerned confers an additional 0.4 cm of height. There are many other genes involved in determining height, such as genes for growth hormone, genes for the receptors on the outside of cells for growth hormone, genes for bone proportion, genes for the timing of the release of hormone and other growth factors. We are born with a genetic potential for height and then the environment exerts its effects as we are growing. So if you had a desire to play pro-basketball but are barely 5 feet 5 inches, don't take this sitting down, blame your misfortune on your genetic makeup and on your mother's health.

Eyesight: Many facets of eyesight are related to your genetic makeup. Macular degeneration is a major cause of blindness. Researchers have found that 16 percent of the macular degeneration patients they tested have mutations in the so-called ABCR gene. If an identical twin has astigmatism, then the other twin has a 60 percent chance of having it as well. Poor eyesight runs in families. If both your parents are nearsighted, then you have about a one in three chance of being nearsighted too. If only one of your parents is nearsighted, then you have a one in five chance of being nearsighted. If neither of your parents is nearsighted, then you have less than a one in forty chance. This would seem to be an obvious case of genetic predisposition. Is it possible that families that read a lot or watch too much TV have a higher chance of having poor eyesight?

A recent twin study suggested that around 90 percent of all nearsightedness and farsightedness involved genes. This doesn't mean that the environment doesn't play a role. It may be that many of these genes increase a person's chances of having bad eyesight but something in the environment has to trigger them. For example, reading, studying, sitting in front of the computer, excessive time playing video games and less time playing outside may all increase the chances of being nearsighted. Genes may be responsible for either making the eye elongated or more malleable and prone to becoming more elongated leading to nearsightedness. When the eye becomes more malleable, nearsightedness is not guaranteed; destructive habits influence your eyesight. Obviously, you will need to ignore this second type of genetic makeup where you carry some responsibility if you want to blame genetics for you needing glasses.

Physical disorders: There are a huge number of disorders and diseases related to genetics. Some examples include neuromuscular disorders, breast cancer, cleft palate, cystic fibrosis, Down syndrome, hemophilia, Huntington's disease, muscular dystrophy, schizophrenia, spina bifida, Marfan syndrome, tay-sachs disease, and XYY syndrome to name a few. There is also a strong genetic component to other disorders including autism, heart disease, hypertension, diabetes, and many cancers. If you suffer from high blood pressure, don't bother changing your diet and bad habits; remember there is a possibility that your hypertension is due, at least in part, to genetics. You can pretend that it is all beyond your control and blame your genome for many other physical disorders. When in doubt, assume a genetic component to any disease or disorder that you have, and blame away.

Samuel occasionally exhibits erratic behavior; going on shopping sprees, obsessing over certain foods, becoming verbally abusive to his wife and their children, wanting to pursue alternative sexual relationships, and threatening to leave his family and move out. He has gone for counseling, and a psychiatrist recommended antidepressant medications as well as lithium, but Samuel refused. He acknowledges that his behavior is hazardous for himself and his marriage. He says that he thinks he has Asperger syndrome and that it is to blame for his behavioral meltdowns. Asperger syndrome is an autistic disorder characterized by abnormalities of social interaction and communication. In further discussion, Samuel admitted that prior to getting married he was bisexual and he would still like to engage in relationships with other men. This has made him increasingly frustrated with his marriage. The fact is that he was never medically diagnosed with Asperger's, graduated at the top of his classes in high school and college, has a successful career, and develops close relationships with many friends. He was hoping that this diagnosis would excuse his unacceptable behavior.

Mental limitations: Heritability ranges from 0 to 1, defined as the proportion of variance in a trait that is attributable to genes. A heritability of 1 means that variation is genetic in origin, while a heritability of 0 indicates no genetic variation. The heritability of IQ has been estimated at anywhere from 0.4 to 0.8. For comparison, adult height heritability has been estimated at 0.8. Other traits like depression demonstrate a low heritability, from 0.29–0.42 (indicating a relatively large environmental influence). But, remember, anything above 0 implies that you can still blame genetics for being depressed!

The majority of the heritable variance in IQ appears to be carried by the general intelligence factor. Destructive mutation of individual genes associated with development can severely affect intelligence. Strangely enough, the heritability of IQ rises from about 20 percent in infancy, to 40 percent in childhood, to as high as 80 percent in adults. Seems ironic; one may expect that genetic influences would become less important as one gains experience and is influenced by environment (nurture) with increasing age. This suggests that the responsible genes do not just make people smarter and able to answer test questions better, but they enhance a person's ability to learn and develop skill-sets that improve their "mental giftedness" throughout their life. So, this is great news for the blamers of the world. Not only can we blame genetic predisposition on our poor IQ tests, but we can also use this blame to explain why we have less drive and ambition to learn and memorize.

Other

The items we can include in our list of blaming targets is ridiculously long. I can't think of anything that is not fair game in the Blame Game. There are no boundaries and no illegitimate targets. So, with that in mind, here is a list of potential blaming targets, many of which you will recognize; if you're experienced at playing the Blame Game, you have utilized these things for some of your own blames.

Animals: "Dog ate my homework," "I had to clean up after the cats," "Goat ate my book report," "Turtle urinated on my term paper," "My Iguana defecated on my math book." We hear these responses from our kids and perhaps used them ourselves when we were in school. Our little furry friends are wonderful blame targets who don't mind the added responsibility or liability. Our pets provide unconditional love, support, and hugs (especially my boa). No matter what we do to them, they rely on us for their food and their care and they will be there for us. When we blame them without their informed, written consent, they don't ever seem to mind.

Two books, both entitled *Blame it on the Dog* are demonstrations of our ability to blame our pets. In one book, a Harlequin romance by Amy Frazier, a new sixty-pound puppy brings havoc into the lives of a woman and her son by chewing up furniture and doing other "puppy things." In the end, he is to blame for helping her find true love. The other dog book, by Jim Dawson, provides an in-depth and entertaining history of the fart. Enough said.

I was late for an appointment the other day because it took longer than I thought it would to clean up some cages at my house. In addition to a large boa, I also have a lizard and some hermit crabs. I was cleaning up these cages and suddenly realized I was late for an appointment across town. As I'm quickly finishing up and getting into the car, the first thing that comes to mind is, "Darn animals. It's their fault that I'm late." Well how wrong is that? They didn't choose to have me buy them. Nor did they decide when would be an appropriate time for me to clean their cages. They didn't promise me that it would only take a certain period of time to clean the cages and that if I started it today by 4:00 p.m. that I would be done on time to make it for my 6:00 p.m. appointment. While they are an easy blame target, similar to the Stranger Blame it may not be completely true that they are responsible for my tardiness.

<u>*Cars*</u>: Cars is a specific term that we should really generalize to all forms of transportation including planes, trains, and automobiles. We typically use these targets when we are late for any type of appointment. In addition, we should add other forms of non-motorized ground transportation such as bicycles, tricycles, and obviously unicycles, snowshoes, and pogo sticks. It is almost worth buying one of those just to provide an excellent blame when I'm late for anything. We have several types of motorized transportation on the ground including mopeds, motorcycles, city buses, maglev trains (which run on magnets), subways, and school buses. When we're on the water we can blame sailboats, steamboats, kayaks, canoes, rafts, hovercrafts, hydrofoils, cruise ships, and ocean liners. In the air, let us not forget helicopters, gliders, hot air balloons, blimps, seaplanes, and of course, the very under-utilized blame target of space shuttles. "Sorry I'm late for my exam Mr. Morris, my space shuttle was late taking off from Mars." Sounds bizarre now, but someday your grandkids will be using this one.

Finally, we have more unusual forms of transportation, especially used in foreign countries that you should be aware of including camel, horse, elephant, sled dogs, rickshaw, tuk-tuks (three-wheeled motorized vehicles with a handlebar), samlors (non-motorized tuk-tuks), gondolas, and vaporettos (large, multi-passenger gondolas). Before traveling to foreign countries, the U.S. State Department recommends that visitors become familiar with alternative forms of transportation in order to provide accurate international blaming targets.

<u>*Skis*</u>: This category is for equipment used for recreation or competition. Examples would be water skis or snow skis, snowboards, bi- cycles, and even running shoes. Every year there are improvements made to shoes and skis and the like to make them lighter, stronger, more aerodynamic, reduce friction, etc. If

you don't have the latest and greatest new developments for a given sport, how can you possibly be expected to compete or even do an adequate job? You are at a decided disadvantage and your equipment is obviously to blame. Your personal performance should not even be assessed or scrutinized without these top-of-the-line accessories. Even if this were the case, there are several other options for blaming targets such as the weather, the conditions, the competition, the phone ringing last night that kept me awake, etc. So, don't let the potential blame removal stop you from buying new equipment.

Information Sources: How often do each of us make statements that are erroneous? We state something or pass on information that we are sure is a fact only to find out later that we were incorrect. While we are trying to educate and edify friends and strangers alike, we may get accused of making up this information or intentionally trying to spread rumors that aren't true. We must look closely as to our sources of information. Where did we find out the stuff that we are passing on to others? Typically we have garnered this knowledge from what we consider to be a reliable source such as books, videos, movies, news-media, and informational pamphlets. Every news station is biased in some way and their facts will be different than those discussed on other news stations. We should be responsible to verify facts before we pass them on to others.

Holidays: Typically a time of happiness, celebrations, and goodwill, the holidays are also rife with blame. The holidays are associated with family and friends and as such, they can be a painful reminder of poor relationships and are to blame for loneliness and depression when we're not invited to that party next door. We can also blame the holidays for reminding us of family members who have passed on and for memories that cannot be relived. Holidays mean food and beverages. We freely blame holidays for our excessive binging and intoxication. "Of course I put on weight, it's the holiday season." Stock market lowers – blame the holidays. Customers trampled in the Walmart store during "Black Friday" – blame the Holiday. Long lines at the retail stores? Of course it's because of the Holidays. Postprandial fatigue and lethargy (excessive sleepiness after eating loads of turkey) – Blame the Holiday. No money to pay my bills in January? Blame the Holidays in December! Speeding tickets, parking tickets, drunk driving tickets – Yes, you can blame the Holidays. Thank God for the Holidays, they provide much needed blaming excuses.

Cameras: I love to take pictures when I'm traveling. I've never studied photography but I have had numerous complements and have received positive feedback on many pictures that I've taken over the years. I've even had one of my photographs take second place in a photo contest. Truth be told, I'm a truly lousy photographer. My technique involves taking several hundred thousand pictures with the camera set on automatic everything. Eventually I get a great picture here and there and toss the rest into the round file. Digital cameras are a heaven-sent gift for me. Prior to this, it would take me more rolls of film than I am willing to admit in order to end up with one or two really nice shots. Of course, when my "other" pictures are seen by anyone, I blame my camera for the poor lighting, poor composition, and poor detailing. This technique can, of course, be generalized to any device that you may use for art or sport, such as your gun in target shooting, your paint brushes if you are an artist, or your drywall knife if you are reconstructing your house. Be creative in your blames, the sky is the limit. By the way, if you need to squint when you are looking at the sky, blame the sun!

Glasses: Sometimes we need help from certain devices or objects to maximize our enjoyment and be able to fully participate in activities of daily living. The devices or objects to which I'm referring are things like eyeglasses and hearing aids. We may have lost some of our ability to hear or we may have become nearsighted or farsighted and attempted to correct these deficiencies. This sets the stage for some perfect inanimate object blames. "I couldn't concentrate because these darn glasses kept slipping off my nose," "I couldn't see the signs clearly because my glasses fogged up," "I am sorry officer, I didn't hear what you were saying, looks like the battery is going dead on my hearing aid." Okay, I'm sure that you've got plenty more to add to my list. Don't neglect the fact that there are other aids that we can take an opportunity to blame such as a "bad hair day"—blame the new hair brush, "trouble eating at the Chinese restaurant"—blame the slippery chop sticks, "bad sunburn after a day at the beach"—cheap sunscreen. Need I say more?

Menstrual Periods: I cannot speak on this next topic from first-hand experience (thank goodness I can blame the Y chromosome for this) and I don't believe that I have met any women who are overly emotional on a monthly cycle corresponding to their menstrual periods. Therefore, I will only discuss what I have read. There is a rare but serious medical disorder called premenstrual syndrome or PMS, which is related to rapidly changing hormone levels. Significant alterations in hormones such as progesterone result in many physiologic and psychologic perturbations including the occasional need to murder your spouse. The lack of menstrual periods in some women may also result in extreme emotional disturbances each month. This is an amazing gender-based opportunity for women to legitimately get away with behaviors and activities in which they would not otherwise be involved…blame PMS. The beauty of this is that it can be accomplished with relative ease, every single month!

As women near the age of menopause, they begin to experience brief episodes of extreme heat. Not surprisingly, with all these internal changes in hormones, hot flashes are also causally-related to emotional difficulties, and women are said to be prone to behavioral outbursts and huge mood swings. Realize that nobody except you (and maybe your hairdresser) knows for sure if you are at that stage in life. So when you are feeling a tad emotional and need a good cry, or to strike your partner with a kitchen utensil, don't forget: Blame hormones.

Let's not forget the men. If things aren't going well at home and you are kicked out of the house after a big fight, during which time the PMS or hot flash blame card is played, this is your opportunity to stay out with the boys a little bit longer and join in the game using the same blame. "Honey, I stayed out late because of the PMS thing. I care greatly about you and wanted to give you the time that you needed to get in touch with your inner self. You were having such a hard time with me yesterday that I thought I'd give you a break today and go out drinking with Charlie after work. No, you don't have to thank me."

Body Parts: After three knee surgeries, foot surgery, elbow surgeries, lower back surgery, cervical neck fusion, and a host of other surgical procedures, I can claim with utmost confidence that my body is not quite what it used to be. I can still spend an hour on an elliptical machine and do a full-gainer off the diving board. However, there are times when I feel old. Here is where it is greatly convenient for me to blame me. Well, parts of me that don't work as well as others— my knees, my back, my brain... Each of us has some type of physical limitation, or at least a little ache or pain, to blame for not winning that race; or for not walking to work, biking to the park, exercising at the gym, or even getting off the couch ... "Honey, could you give me a hand getting the remote from the coffee table?"

Age: There is not a perfect age. We have not given up hope to find the Fountain of Youth, although now we seem to look for it in syringes, bottles, and operating rooms. Children can't get into PG-13 or R-rated movies. Children also can't enjoy certain rides at amusement parks, or sit in the front seat of modern cars with air bags. "I'm not old enough to do that!" "If I were older, they wouldn't talk to me like that." "If I were older, they wouldn't make me dress like this." This is the age-old age blame. Fortunately for those of us near or beyond the middle of the time-line, the age blame is not unidirectional. There are many self-imposed limitations for which we blame our "elder status": listening to certain music, attending concerts, going to certain dining establishments or parties, sailing on specific cruise ships, movies, amusement parks, skydiving, skiing, and perhaps bull-riding. There are many activities that we would be capable of and enjoy doing but are unwilling to try, either because of fear of failing or fear of stepping out of societal norms. Instead of "going for it," we go without it, blaming it on age.

Now, adolescence and young adulthood are great blaming ages. This is a time when a teenager can take full advantage of their age by appreciating that they are both too old and too young for most things in which they would like to become involved. This results in a lot of prime blaming opportunities. They are too young to stay out all night and be responsible for themselves, yet they are too old to get allowance and extra spending money when they do go out. They are too young to participate in some extreme sports, yet they are too old to participate in some child-like activities; too young for some movies and too old for other movies; too young for some books and too old for other books; too young for some conversations and too old for other conversations; too young to wear certain types of clothes and too old to wear others. Yes, the perfect blaming age.

Fictitious Characters: In 2014, two 12-year old girls in Wisconsin savagely attacked a classmate, stabbing her 19 times and bringing her within inches of ending her life. Who's to blame for this brutal assault? Let's take a look at the usual suspects.

1) *Mental illness.* Many homicides and attempted homicides of implicate mental illness. The perpetrator typically has a history of erratic behavior, psychological disease, or disturbed thought patterns so blatant that it surprising they were ignored prior to the event. In this case, the two girls plotted together for weeks as to how they would carry out this plan. They appeared to understand that stabbing someone with a knife had the potential to kill them, which they stated was their goal. Their plan was allegedly quite detailed and well thought out. We have no knowledge that either of these girls had a history of psychological illness or trauma.

2) *The victim.* When someone inflicts harm on another, we often look to the victim to assign some blame. What were they wearing, what did he or she say or do that would inspire such negative passions? In this case, the victim was not someone whom we believe had wronged either of the girls or posted photos of them on the Internet. She was not just a classmate, but was described as a "friend". Thus, labeling the victim as the causative agent may be impossible in this case.

3) *The weapon.* If the weapon had been a gun rather than a knife, this would be an easy answer. We would hear cries for more gun regulation and better gun laws. The anti-gun lobbyists would argue that having the inspiration to kill someone would not be of significant concern if there were no access to guns. But the weapon in this case was a knife. What do we do about a

knife? Should we open up the discussion to banning knives? New knife laws and stricter knife regulations? I work in a trauma center and have personally cared for patients impaled by forks. Should we institute a law in which only adults should be allowed to use metal kitchen utensils? The conversation sounds ridiculous in this framework, yet in the light of the gun discussions, it's worth mentioning. The variety of improvisational weapons available to anyone wanting to do harm to others is mind-boggling. If you believe that guns are to blame for recent attacks at schools, then you must be consistent in your contention and attribute this attempted homicide to knives.

4) *Religion.* Many homicides, are attributed to religious disparities: Fort Hood and Boston Marathon to name a few. Anti-Semitism is on the rise. There have been attacks against Sikhs in Wisconsin. Christian Zealots have assaulted pro-abortionists. Religion-inspired assaults are common enough that we must eliminate this motive before moving on to other reasons. In this case, we have no knowledge of any religious motivations or radicalism which may have stirred emotions leading to this crime.

5) *Politics.* Political ideologies inspire passion and emotions. They also typically inspire conflict and occasionally violence. There are no political parties that are innocent in this behalf. However, we have no knowledge, at this time, that the girls involved in this attack were motivated by religious beliefs.

6) *Slender Man.* Television, Internet, porn sites, video games, x-box, and motion picture movies. These are well-known contributors to the increase in societal violence. We, especially teenagers and young adults, are often negatively influenced by violent multi-media. The majority of comments on the news and Internet reflect on the negative influence of Slender Man and the power of online horror sites, games, and apps. What does Slender Man have to do with this attempted murder? The pre-teens who committed this crime said that they were inspired to do so out of a desire to be proxies of Slender Man and live with him in his mansion. If you are older than 16 years, you may not have been previously exposed to Slender Man.

He's a fictitious character that has garnered millions of Internet fans through horror and fantasy websites such as CreepyPasta. Slender Man has become the inspiration for multiple horror stories, phone apps, and online games. One such video has more than 11 million page hits! These girls may not have fully understood that Slender Man is not a real person and appear to have been influenced by some of the stories. There are already calls for banning Slender Man.

7) *Parents.* Unlike most of the homicides in which we have thus far faced, the attackers in this case were not teens. They are pre-teens! Yet, there are no Internet police monitoring and verifying the age of participants. Consequently, we are left to our own accord to monitor, oversee, and supervise our children. As a father, I know this is a difficult, but necessary undertaking. It is most unfortunate that it often takes a tragic event such as this to remind us of our awesome responsibility to communicate with our children. As a consequence of this gruesome attack, I had the opportunity to discuss Slender Man with my own children. I learned that my youngest daughter (15 years old) had tried one of the Slender Man games on a friend's phone. She said that it was odd, scary and didn't appeal to her. I am hopeful that these sorts of heart-rending situations will inspire similar conversations between all parents and their children. Does this mean that a caring and involved parent, even a helicopter mother, is solely accountable for what their pre-teen children do? No. There is shared responsibility. As parents, we need to be involved in our childrens' lives, but we can't control every aspect of their behavior at all times.

8) *Age.* These children committed a heinous crime. Yet, they are children. When are they responsible and accountable for their actions? Younger and younger children are being tried in court as adults. At what age should we expect children to be morally and ethically responsible for their actions and behaviors? By age 3 or 4, children typically understand right from wrong, however, parents still represent a child's external conscience. Children stop doing something wrong because they know that parents are there. By age 6, children develop an internal conscience and moral sense. By age 7-8 there's an adherence to

rules and by age 10, children understand more about societal rules and that they may be negotiated. It is also at this stage (10-12 years old) that children develop rational, logically thought and begin to understand how their actions may affect others. The formal operational stage (from Piaget) begins at about 12 years of age. These early adolescents start to think hypothetically: assessing consequences of their actions without actually experiencing them. They consider several possibilities and plan their actions based on potential outcomes. At about 12 years of age is also where children begin to consider the perspectives of others. They become more independent and create social identities through group interactions, engaging in activities for intense emotional experiences. So, where does this information leave us?

9) These girls committed the crime and are thus, responsible, in some respect. Whether they are morally, ethically, and criminally responsible as legal adults, will be the subject of much more debate. While they most likely know right from wrong, their cognitive development is not yet fully mature. With this in mind, it would be easier to blame it all on Slender Man.

One final note to conclude this chapter: There are some individuals that are opposed to blaming inanimate objects and abstract constructions. Albert Einstein stated, "You can't blame gravity for falling in love." Jose Canseco is opposed to blaming medications, asking, "Are we to say that any individual who's on steroids that has an angry moment is due to steroids?" Nikolai Gogol warned, "It is no use to blame the looking glass if your face is awry." There are also those who would like to be able to blame things but have not yet perfected the art of blaming. The actress Delta Burke was one such person. "I wish I could blame it on the choreography, but it's not a musical. I just had a clumsy moment." Practice makes perfect—both in terms of dancing and blaming!

8. Governmental Blame

"Let us not seek the Republican answer or the Democratic answer, but the right answer. Let us not seek to fix the blame for the past. Let us accept our own responsibility for the future."

John F. Kennedy

It's hard to not blame the government. After all the government is so intimately involved in so many varied aspects of our lives. Blaming the government would actually fit in the previous "what" chapter, however, governmental blame is so prevalent and there is so much material, that I needed to create a separate chapter for this. When we say, "The government", we mean the government in general and everyone who works for or represents the government. For purposes of blaming, individuals working with the government, while they are performing their jobs, are classified as "what"s rather than "who"s. When we blame them, we blame "the government" and not specifically individuals working in the government.

Elections

Members of a democratic society occasionally blame their government for societal problems. It is understandable that people would blame an autocratic, military, or even parliamentary government for which they did not have an opportunity to vote. Many in the United States believe that we live in a democratic society. We believe that we elect government officials to represent our needs and perhaps even our wants and desires. Government of the people, by the people, and for the people. Or so we think.

In reality, the United States government is a federal republic set up by the Constitution and adopted by the Constitutional Convention of 1787. The executive branch, consisting of the president and vice- president, with the help of an appointed cabinet, conducts the administrative business of the country. The legislative branch, or Congress, consists of the Senate and the House of Representatives, the members of which are directly elected to represent us. However, the executive branch is *chosen* by a 538-member Electoral College.

To be elected to the executive branch, candidates must attain an absolute majority in the Electoral College. Although these Electors from the College are themselves elected to vote for the people of a given state, many of these Electors are "Super Delegates" or "Unpledged Electors" who can vote for whomever they personally choose. Some will even break their pledge, voting for a candidate other than the one voted for by the state majority. Thus, as became apparent in 2000, we can elect a president, with a minority of the population. When we examine this more closely, it is apparent that we always elect a president with a minority of the population. It's the percentage of eligible voters who show up to the polls that count.

This loss of power to control our government is more than made up for in the power that we gain in blaming ability. This loss of control in the election process as well as the inability to control how our elected and appointed representatives vote on specific issues (except by the threat of non re-election) gives us the freedom to blame even those for whom we did vote. In a speech in 1982, President Reagan blamed those who blamed him for the failing economy, "In recent weeks, a lot of people have been playing what I call the Blame Game." How popular is that when a standing U.S. president promotes a game? Blaming people for blaming? Auto-blaming. What was the result of his speech? An article from James Reston of the *New York Times* titled "The Blame Game." In it he said, "The president's speech was a clever and brilliant example of 'the blame game'. The whole thrust of it was to avoid responsibility for the economic recession and unemployment, and to blame the Democrats in particular and the tragedy of history in general." Wow, short turnaround time for blaming the blamer.

We have a section of the government known as the judicial branch. These judges-for-life interpret the laws of the land and provide binding opinions regarding important legislation and disputes. When their decisions are not in keeping with our own view of the world or the U.S. Constitution, we must try to keep in mind that these individuals do not stand alone. They are appointed by the president of the United States and he (or someday she) must also share any blames directed toward the Supreme Court.

It is difficult to find people that are satisfied with their local or federal government at any particular time. While Governmental Blaming occurs continuously, it is particularly prevalent during presidential or congressional election years. There is not an election speech delivered that does not include at least five blames of the current government or opposing candidates; these, of course, are typically Subtle Blames. I refer you to the article in *BQ* magazine titled, "Find the Blames—Election Politics, Subtle Yet Potent." The article describes how difficult it may be to locate all the Subtle Blames in an election campaign speech and how polished the candidates become at delivering them, often without any blatant attacks. During times of recession, depression, or obvious difficulties for which the government is readily acknowledged to be responsible, Blatant Blaming is acceptable. A large component of what is commonly referred to as "negative campaigning" is, in fact, Governmental Blaming.

The people of the United States endured twenty months of blaming and campaigning from 2006 through 2008. By the time the presidential candidates, the legislative candidates, and the news media were finished, over 5 billion dollars was spent and there was not a stone left unblamed. It is interesting to observe how blaming patterns change during the course of an election. Liberals blame Conservatives, Conservatives blame Liberals, and Libertarians blame everyone. The news media becomes a representative of the government during election years and takes on responsibility by endorsing candidates and demonstrating bias in reporting. For example, the conservative-leaning Fox News, while "fair and balanced," clearly supported Republican candidates, while MSNBC heavily advertised for the Democratic Party and ac- cording to MSNBC, Barack Obama could do no wrong. This allows us to associate each news station, newspaper, and reporter with a particular candidate, or at least a party.

Once we place a label, then we are free to include them with our blame of the government. The most blatant of this over the past few years has been MSNBC, which endorsed President Obama. Even though Obama was popularly elected, MSNBC was not and lost in the ratings due to their lack of objectivity and frequent Blatant Blames toward the Conservative side of the fence. Of course MSNBC blamed Republicans and Fox News for creating and supporting destructive policies which led to a poor economy in which people couldn't afford to watch MSNBC. Meanwhile many in the conservative movement blamed the liberal media for unprecedented political bias.

During the presidential primaries, each candidate blames the other candidates from their own party for the way that they dealt with some facet of business or government. It's every man or woman for themselves. They become more entangled in this web of blame and typically accusations transition from Subtle to Blatant. Every candidate blames every other candidate for something. After the primary season, the candidates who have withdrawn from the race develop a respect for their party's nominee. They stop blaming and provide a much appreciated endorsement, vie for a position in their cabinet, and initiate blaming of the opposing party's nominee, who until this time had been mostly forgotten.

Senator Hillary Clinton who was at one point the front-runner for the Democratic Party, was very critical for many months of her opponent Barack Obama. Another very critical and outspoken opponent of Obama was his current vice-president, Joe Biden. During the primary campaign, both Mr. Biden and Ms. Clinton stated that Barack Obama was not prepared to be the president of the United States. Of course, as soon as Barack Obama became the Democratic nominee, he was praised by all in his party. The troops were gathered and they rallied behind their candidate after changing their minds about his credentials. Now, John McCain and President George Bush became the target of blame for the country's ills. Of course, early in the presidential race, Republicans blamed John McCain for stances and legislation that some considered very "left- leaning" in the Republican Party. After he became the nominee, as in the Democratic Party, many of his blamers became his supporters.

As the primaries raged on for the 2008 elections, former President Bill Clinton, in support of Hillary, focused on Barak Obama and went on a blaming trail accusing the senator of bringing "race" into the race. Interparty blaming wasn't just a Democratic event. Conservatives blamed John McCain for his liberal views, policies, and voting records. So, with the candidates not dedicating as much time as they needed to blame the other party, the news media took over. The liberal media praised John McCain for his voting record and his moderate stance and blamed Conservatives for not supporting him.

The conservative media blamed Hillary Clinton for her senatorial voting record and blamed President Obama for his lack of voting record. Following the primary election, the liberal news media switched gears from praising John McCain and blaming Conservatives to associating John McCain with Conservatives and including him in the "big blame." John McCain became George Bush's look-alike and thus deserved all the blame that was afforded President Bush.

National Debt

When should a United States president consider the state of the country their responsibility? One year after taking office President Obama and his staff continue to blame former President Bush for ongoing issues in national security, the economy and the United States reputation abroad. In his 2010, State of the Union address, President Obama focused on blaming Bush. "By the time I took office, we had a one year deficit of over $1 trillion and projected deficits of $8 trillion over the next decade. Most of this was the result of not paying for two wars, two tax cuts, and an expensive prescription drug program. On top of that, the effects of the recession put a $3 trillion hole in our budget. All this was before I walked in the door." At which point, Senator John McCain turned to Senator Lindsey Graham and mouthed the words, "Blame it on Bush." Should we ignore the fact that as a senator, President Obama voted for the stimulus package and then contributed to that deficit with his own $787 billion stimulus package and other programs? The Presidential Blame Game is wearing thin with the country's patience. It hardly replaces the leadership needed to drive the country out of a recession.

Now that Obama has been in power for six years, is the National Debt coming under better control? Hardly, the debt has exponentially risen to over $18 trillion. Without pointing any fingers, here are some fun facts about the debt:

1. The debt is about 140% of our personal disposable income, 190% of our per capita income, and 104% of the Gross Domestic Product. These are all the highest in the history of this country.
2. The national debt is increasing by about $35 million per hour – around $2 billion every day!
3. Celebrity Tom Cruise made about $75 million in 2013. For him to earn $18 trillion, he would have had to make $75 million a year…for the next 240,000 years.
4. If you like to shop, you would have to spend $5 million a day…for the next 9,863 years to spend $18 trillion.
5. A stack of 18 trillion dollar bills would reach upwards of over 1 million miles.
6. If you spent $1 million a day since the year 0, you would not have spent $1 trillion by now!
7. It took 39 presidents and 200 years for the debt to reach $1 trillion. By the time President Clinton left the White House (20 yrs after Reagan took office) the debt had reached $5.6 trillion. Eight years later, under Bush II, the debt had almost doubled to $10.7 trillion. After six years of Obama, another $8 trillion has been added so far. Just as Reagan, Bush, and Clinton were responsible for the debt, so is Obama. Responsibility is blind to party affiliation!

Fast forward to 2014, unfortunately, not much has changed. The answer to the question of when does the state of the country become Mr. Obama's responsibility is still up in the air. Not only is the goal to redistribute wealth, but to equally distribute blame. Not unlike other politicians, claiming credit for successes seems to be his individual right. In contrast, when things go badly, it's Bush, it's Fox News, it's House Republicans, it's his underlings…As syndicated columnist Cal Thomas has written, "Blaming others for one's failure is not a strategy for victory. It's what losers do."

Security

In 2008, Mr. Obama blamed President George Bush for believing bad intelligence about Iraq's Saddam Hussein's possession of weapons of mass destruction. Yet, in 2014, when he erroneously referred to the Islamic terrorist group, ISIS as "JV" – junior varsity, Obama blamed his Defense Intelligence Agency Chief, James Clapper.

Between the years 2010 and 2014, President Obama can be seen on more than 25 videos specifically stating that he did not have the power or legal authority to unilaterally change the immigration system – that was the job of congress. He said to do that he would have to be an "Emperor". Yet, in 2014, blaming the Republican congress for lack of action, he told the American people that he now had legal authority to change the immigration system. Sounds like we have an Emperor.

Obamacare

Potentially one of the greatest blames of the decade arose in 2014 with what has also been called the greatest lie of the year. Obama, many in his administration and several democrats claimed, "If you like your doctor, you can keep your doctor. If you like your plan, you can keep your plan." We then found out was this was not true, Obama defended, don't blame me. I didn't know that. Then we discovered that the administration indeed did know ahead of time that keeping your doctor and your plan was not going to be possible. MIT Economics Professor Jonathan Gruber was initially the golden boy and highly paid consultant (about $7 million) for the new Healthcare reform bill. He was specifically referred to by Mr. Obama and Nancy Pellosi prior to the bill passing. Recently, multiple videos have surfaced in which Professor Gruber discusses the Healthcare bill. He admits that it was written and presented in such a way as to con (lie to) the "stupid" American public so they would be excited about the law. The Obama administration and democratic senators now blame Gruber – who they no longer admit to knowing.

Moreover Obamacare – the unaffordable care act, involved the worst website enrollment in the history of website enrollments. After months of blaming and finger pointing as to who was ultimately responsible, Kathleen Sebelius, the Secretary of Health & Human Services was put up on the chopping block. She admitted to nothing, yet resigned from her administrative role. Once again, Obama escaped responsibility – the buck did not stop there!

From October 1st through the 16th, 2013, the Federal Government shutdown. Congress failed to enact legislation either appropriating funds for the fiscal year or a continuing resolution to "kick the can down the road" with an interim appropriations bill. This was the third longest government shutdown in US history. Who was to blame for this occurring? Heated political fighting between the Republican-led House of Representatives which attempted to defund Obamacare and President Obama with the Democratic-led Senate who wanted to maintain funding, led to a budget impasse. While many were dismayed by the government shutdown, I was personally relieved during the 16 day-long shutdown and would have been okay with another week or two. While they weren't working, they weren't wasting quite as much of our money. Besides, the political blamefest was quite entertaining.

Internal Revenue Service

In 2013, the US Internal Revenue Service (IRS) admitted to targeting selected political groups applying for tax-exempt status. The groups were almost exclusively conservative and right-wing-leaning. This revelation resulted in several investigations including one by the FBI and by the Attorney General. It also caused an endless supply of blames. Unanimously it was agreed that this was an abuse of power.

Conservatives and Republicans blamed the IRS for politically-motivated targeting. They blamed the Obama administration, who may have had knowledge of the impropriety and did not release the information until after the Presidential election. They also blamed the media for attempting to bury the scandal. Liberals and Democrats blamed the Republicans for trying to make a scandal out of what they felt was innocent irregular behavior. Some IRS officials blamed the White House for giving it direction. Several IRS administrators left their jobs during and after the investigation, including Lois Lerner, the IRS figure at the center of this controversy. Incidentally, Ms. Lerner blamed her computer for the loss of many emails related to this scandal. In November, 2014, these emails magically reappeared.

What else do we know about the IRS? Between 2010 and 2012, the IRS spent *$50 million* on conferences, including $4 million for one conference alone. In one year, top IRS Officials spent $9.5 million on travel in private jets. Benefits included baseball tickets and stays in $3,500 per night Presidential suites. Obama blamed some IRS administrators who were subsequently replaced.

Privacy Violations

In the summer of 2013, we learned that for years, the federal government has been gathering information about us. Not just information, but phone records, internet data from private companies, and video chats. We, the people blamed Obama and the Congress. Even though this violation predates Obama, he promised transparency and criticized Bush for similar actions. Violating the privacy rights of all American citizens? In part we are to blame for not limiting Congress.

Entitlements

Of course, our Governmental Blame doesn't start or end at the national level. We have plenty of opportunity to blame state, county, and local city officials for a multitude of policies. Everything including road repair, snow removal, building permits, pet permits, house permits, property taxes, school taxes, income tax rates, itemized deductions, and 540,362 other important aspects of our daily life are under control of some governmental agency that has been, currently is, or someday will be the target of your blame of the day.

Now is the "Age of Entitlement." We are told by many in the government that anyone and everyone who wants to own a house, a car, or buy on credit deserves those things because we live in the U.S.A. Whether you can afford these items, have good credit, or have a job is not as important as actually having stuff. We are told that it is better that the government "bail out" companies and individuals who have made bad decisions than to let them fail. We are setting up a system of entitlement where it becomes legitimate to blame the government for all those things that they have promised us or said that we should have. I can blame the government for not making my mortgage payment and for me having to rent an apartment.

In 2010, the government let it be known that tax rates were going up on the wealthiest 2 percent of the population. Obviously, those 2 percent, who were already paying a great deal of the tax burden in the country, are not doing their "fair" share and are certainly to blame for the unemployed not getting jobs and for the state of the economy. So, right now we can blame the rich. But when the government starts to tax the rich about 60 percent of their income and uses (wastes?) returns on poorly run government programs, this may lead to fewer jobs, as the wealthy can't afford to grow their businesses. When the wealthy have less money to donate to needy charities, who should we then blame? The government has proposed limiting tax deductions received for charitable donations. This would bring the government an estimated $630 billion dollars to waste (err, I meant *use*). So, if people are truly sincere about their need to give to the poor, it shouldn't matter what the tax implications are, right? However, when we see Warren Buffet lose 60 percent of his wealth in a year due to a huge economic decline, and thousands of the nation's wealthiest people losing billions of dollars to Bernie Madoff's Ponzi scheme, I don't know if it's right to blame them for not wanting to throw money at inefficient government or for not having enough money left to donate to charities.

When the government takes more money in from wealthy, productive, job-creating members of our society to give out checks to those who choose not to seek or report gainful employment and thus do not pay taxes, is it appropriate to blame the individuals who are being entitled or is it now truly the government's responsibility by promoting a welfare state? I am not saying that anyone who doesn't pay taxes shouldn't be given government money. There are millions of examples of people who are unable to work or find jobs and are in need of welfare. These are not the people to whom I am referring. I am directing this at people who choose not to take control of and responsibility for their lives and want to blame the government for not supporting them in their beliefs.

The bluest of blue states, Massachusetts elected conservative Republican, Scott Brown over Democratic candidate, Martha Coakley in January, 2010. The internet and other forms of media were replete with blaming articles. Laurie Kellman, of the Associated Press wrote, *Democrats Play Blame Game for Mass. Senate Loss* (http://labs.daylife.com/journalist/laurie_kellman).

Washington insiders and Obama allies were quick to blame the candidate herself for losing the race for the "Kennedy seat". The Coakley camp returned fire by accusing the national Democratic Party and the Democratic Senatorial Campaign Committee for not helping out earlier and doing a better job energizing the base. The Coakley campaign also blamed the loss on public frustration with the Obama administration's stance on health care and on the failure of the administration to prevent the attempted Christmas Day bombing of a Detroit-bound airliner. Republicans blamed President Obama for focusing on health care reform rather than the economy. To top it off in a Blatant Blame, former Governor and Presidential candidate, Howard Dean actually blamed former President George Bush for the Senatorial loss. President Obama similarly stated that the loss was due to the public's dissatisfaction with the last *eight years* of government policies and lack of change.

9. Problems With The Game

"If you keep saying things are going to be bad, you have a good chance of being a prophet."

Isaac Bashevis Singer

Up until now The Game seems like an unbelievably great deal; phenomenally popular, relatively easy to learn, play it anywhere and with anyone, requires little set-up time, and the instructions are simple. What more could you want in a game? On the surface the Blame Game is lots of fun and a worthwhile way to spend your afternoon. However, there is much that I haven't told you about the Game that may influence your decision about where, when, how often, and with whom you want to play.

Not fun... especially for the blamee

Most of this book is about the blamer. Why to blame, how to do it properly, etc. We can't completely ignore the person or thing being blamed; the blamee, the blamed, the TOB (the target of blame), the scapegoat, the stooge, the donkey. The Blame Game is not the be all and end all for people at the receiving end of the blaming whip.

If the TOB is God, God has not, does not, and will not be dramatically affected by being the target of your blame. That doesn't, however, mean that you won't damage your relationship with a supreme being. Similarly, nature, like God, will be able to deal with all the accusations and finger-pointing. As a matter of fact, as many of you may already realize, when you blame nature it often retaliates and gives you more of the same (i.e., "don't fool with mother nature").

Animals rarely speak up and defend themselves. They do not want to call attention to the fact that they were considered the cause of something bad or evil. But they are psychologically and emotionally injured by being the victims of blame. It may lead to visits with the dog whisperer in an attempt to clean up the residual emotional garbage.

Blaming inanimate objects such as rocks and cars and vacuum cleaners may seem atraumatic to you. However, the Inanimate Objects Foundation, established to protect the rights of these mistreated items, has issued this mission statement: "To deter humankind from blaming us for their own misgivings or bad fortune." Even inert, inorganic matter matters.

Finally, a few words about humans; they don't like to be blamed. It results in emotional and psychological injury. Living in a blaming culture makes us fear being blamed and inhibits what we say, what we think, what we do, and how we act. This phenomenon manifests itself in several different ways including: physicians who won't try to help people outside of a hospital fear being sued; people who witness and ignore crimes being committed fear retribution; individuals who don't want to take on new responsibilities at work and are inhibited from achieving success because of a fear of being blamed for failure.

It's expensive

The Blame Game is not free. It's in the fine print. When you're purchasing a plane ticket on Orbitz or subscribing to a new cell phone plan, do you actually read the entire agreement? Pete Seeger, an American Folk Singer and Political Activist wrote, *"Education is when you read the fine print. Experience is what you get if you don't."*

I rented a car for a week in Orlando, Florida. I was told the price for the rental was about $270. As I was taking a large family with luggage, I upgraded to a larger minivan for a few extra dollars per day. At the end of the week, I was returning the car and almost fell over when I saw the bill. There were fees and charges and taxes and taxes on fees and taxes on charges, and taxes on taxes. The rental bill had more than tripled from what I was expecting. When I questioned some of the numbers, I was told that I had signed the rental agreement. The agent curtly told me, "If you don't like what we're giving you, you should have read the contract more closely. You have no one to blame but yourself." … She was right! Well, after playing the Blame Game for several years, I certainly have had many experiences related to the high costs of the blame game. The Game has many hidden costs. The costs of blaming are often deferred and are usually not truly realized by the participants. There is no detailed cost analysis provided to the players prior to purchasing this game. Some typical costs of purchasing the game involve losing control over your life, poor relationships with family and friends, worsening your view of other people, and limiting your potential for success. As compared to the cost of my collector's edition of Monopoly ($39), the price for participating in the Blame Game is outrageous!

You could be wrong

There are many reasons why our blaming may be misdirected or inappropriately applied, unless of course we are intentionally using Deceitful Blames and knowingly committing Blaming fraud. Even if you are 100 percent sure in your belief that another person or thing is to blame, you might still be wrong! That's the point; you can never be 100 percent sure. We rely on our senses but they are not always correct. There are numerous cases of wrong identity, wrong person, overheard misinformation, and wrong assumptions inferred, due to faulty or missing information. Paul Harvey would say, "Now for the rest of the story." The rest of the story is the part that the blamer didn't hear or misheard or misunderstood. It is the most important part of the story making the whole blame an untruth.

    I was teaching a self-defense class several years ago. There was one young boy who used to attend class regularly. He was very bright and very shy. After several months, he built up his confidence, made many friends and was becoming quite proficient. He took the summer off to go to camp, and when he returned, the billing service did not put him back in the computer to start collecting payments again. After several months of free lessons, they realized that this family had not been paying anything. I said that "since it was our fault, they shouldn't have to pay for what he already attended, let's just start again next month." However, in re-entering data, the billing service billed the family for four months.

My student's father left a voice mail, outraged that I would try to pull one over on him like this. The voicemail was blaming. I called back to explain what happened and pointed out that while this was indeed our error, his son had attended class regularly for six months free of charge. I told him that it was our mistake for which he would not incur any charges. He apologized for the misunderstanding and proceeded to tell me how much his son loved the classes and how much they had helped him in school and at home. The next day this father called me back and said that his son was not going to be coming to class anymore. Apparently, he had overheard his father leave the voice message and all of the not-so- nice things that he said about me. He told his father that he didn't want to take lessons from someone like that. His father was not able to convince him that it was all a misunderstanding resulting in lots of blame.

It is hard for us to acknowledge that we might be wrong; we often demand perfection of others. We believe that we have such a great understanding of the information from our senses that we can make solid conclusions upon which to blame others. How many times have you felt hurt, angry, or humiliated because you either made assumptions or read into something that wasn't there or wasn't intended? When you learn the rest of the story, it is usually an embarrassing situation begging for an apology.

I was at a conference years ago having dinner with a colleague. He said that he had run into an old classmate, and when he waved and said hello he was acknowledged with only a slight nod and barely a smile. While he was relating this story to me, he looked up and pointed across the room, "There he is now!" The ex-classmate happened to be sitting at a table on the opposite side of the room. I told him that he should give it another attempt. So my friend got up and went to the restroom passing close to his classmate's table and waved.

My friend returned to our table and was upset; again no

response. He tried to figure out what he had done to deserve that kind of treatment. His classmate was "stuck-up and unfriendly," he said. I convinced him to confront the classmate about what might be going on. After about fifteen minutes at the other table, he re- turned and said, "Guess what? Wrong guy! It wasn't who I thought it was." He told me that the look-alike was a nice guy who does some similar research and they exchanged contact information.

Hinders relationships

"You did this to me!" "This is your fault!" "If it wasn't for you I could have been a somebody!" These statements won't end a biologic relationship, but as with blaming, criticizing, disrespecting, accusing, contempt, and condemning, they are not great ways to make friends and influence people.

Blaming erects verbal walls around us; occasionally protecting, often isolating. Blaming is often fear-based. Fear of success. Fear of failure. Fear of winning. Fear of losing. Relationships, whether they are with friends, relatives, lovers, or business partners, must be based on trust and respect, not fear. Blaming leads to a decreased desire to communicate and a sense of powerlessness; two qualities that don't lend themselves to developing close bonds with others. Even those who you are not blaming develop a lack of trust when they hear you accusing others. This general sense of distrust is damaging to everyone's ability to form close bonds with those around them.

Relies on negativity

Negative thoughts initiate blaming. You can't blame without thinking negative thoughts. Negative thoughts begin as seedlings and mature like floral bulbs in well-nurtured soil. Negative thoughts aren't comfortable just being thoughts. They float around in your brain looking for a way out, and they do this by becoming negative words. Negative words, such as those involved in blaming, put negativity and bad energy into the universe. Whether you believe in God, a god, an ethereal energy, yin and yang, or *The Secret*, all of our thoughts, words, and energies affect others and influence things and people in ways that we often don't and can't appreciate.

When you start thinking about a talk that you have to give at a big business meeting, your blood pressure elevates, your heart rate accelerates, and you start to sweat. These symptoms are real. The fact that they happened because of your thoughts doesn't make them less real; but they were avoidable. We injure ourselves by these negative thoughts and ideas.

How often have we wounded ourselves by getting angry, jealous, vengeful, or fearful? These negative thoughts, ideas, and attitudes negatively influence our behavior and the feelings of those that we're close to. Unhappy people are filled with strong criticisms of everyone and everything. Everyone else is to blame. Negative attitudes fill us with discontent, not leaving enough room for happiness and contentment. Negative people drain energy of those around them. When you listen to someone who is constantly blaming others, you wonder what they are saying about you when you are not around. It breeds distrust and creates a growing spiral of cynicism.

10. Benefits of Quitting

"All blame is a waste of time. No matter how much fault you find with another, and regardless of how much you blame him, it will not change you. The only thing blame does is to keep the focus off you when you are looking for external reasons to explain your unhappiness or frustration. You may succeed in making another feel guilty about something by blaming him, but you won't succeed in changing whatever it is about you that is making you unhappy."

Dr. Wayne Dyer

I've described problems that can happen when you blame. I've discussed trying to decrease negativity by less Blame Game playing time. But we are better than that. We should not be about decreasing negativity. Decreasing negativity is good. Enhancing positivity is better. Positive people have a positive outlook on life — irrespective of the apparent failures, successes, or external events that affect each of us. Quitting the Blame Game is your first step to gaining control of your life, helping to achieve and actualize your potential, being more successful at work, helping your marriage and other relationships. Stepping off the blame train will help you make new friends and gain respect from old ones. You'll live longer, happier, and healthier.

More control of your life

The person who is verbally attacking others with a blame may be labeled "the attacker" and the blamee is "the victim." However, by blaming others and trying to justify why it's not your fault, you also become a victim. You are saying, "I have no control over this. Someone else controls what I think, and the way I feel and behave." While you are relinquishing responsibility for your actions and behavior, you are being self-victimized by the act of blaming. Whether you are blaming someone for your own mistakes or for unpleasant things that you believe are happening to you, having someone or something to blame for your mistakes will not alleviate your problems; but rather it will provide them with a firm foundation.

Most people are tired during the day. Why? Life is draining, work is draining, school is draining, friends and family are draining, you're overworked and underpaid, not getting enough sleep, etc. Well, how can we go about trying to be less tired? We can change our work or home schedule to get more sleep, our job situation to achieve more satisfaction, our after-work activities to decrease energy expenditure or our night-time behaviors to have a more restful sleep. Alternatively, we could keep everything the way it is, save the time and energy that it would cost to make effective changes, blame all of those external factors and conclude by saying, "It's not my fault!"

Here's another option. Mononucleosis is an infectious viral disease caused by the Ebstein-Barr virus (EBV) and characterized by fever, sore throat, muscle soreness, and fatigue. The fatigue often lasts one to two months, yet the virus can remain dormant in cells indefinitely and resurface later. Some adults present with tiredness, depression, lymph node swelling, and fever for months or years and are diagnosed with chronic fatigue syndrome (CFS).

While no causative link to EBV has been proven, the Center for Disease Control tells us that chronic fatigue states occur in 10 percent of those who contract mononucleosis. Luckily, almost all of us have had EBV/mononucleosis infections, so when you are really tired, worn out, and somewhat depressed by a situation, blame EBV.

Several years ago I had some close friends diagnosed with CFS. This was great for them because they now had something to blame on their tiredness. They felt better at first with the realization that they were personally not to blame and they were not, in fact, lazy. They became victims of the disease and removed the possibility that they could control their destiny. While no cures for CFS exist, my friends are somehow no longer afflicted with this disease.

Alternative medicine practitioners also began diagnosing tired and depressed patients with vitamin, mineral, and nutrient deficiencies to explain many of their complaints and behaviors. The list of vitamins and minerals for treatment includes: vitamins A, B, C, D, and E, calcium, magnesium, iron, and potassium. There is also a huge list of other enzymes and nutrients that have been proposed as associated with fatigue, that we are able to blame for our lack of energy. Any one of these may be a factor in explaining why we are tired on any given day. But at the end of that day, you can sit on the couch with your potato chips and the remote control between your toes, complaining about your malic acid deficiency or you can take control of your actions, find motivation from within and get off your tush. Even if you are truly afflicted by a disease or illness or there is an identifiable cause for your attitude, behavior, and sentiment, blaming this as a source of your woes excuses you from trying to fix the problem.

Here is the truth. **You have control.** You have control over so much more of your life, jobs, and relationships than you will ever realize or admit to. We so often confuse needs and wants. We go to our chosen place of work because we want to, not because we need to. Yes, it would be difficult, but we could change jobs or downsize our houses or move into an apartment. We may not want to do this but it is our choice. When you quit blaming and take responsibility for yourself, you begin to see so many more needs as wants. When this transition occurs, your choices become endless and for the first time in your life you can start to control your present, your future, and your destiny.

Better Mental Health

We often blame others when we search for reasons to explain our frustration, anxiety, or depression. You may succeed in making someone feel guilty, but you won't succeed in curing your unhappiness. You are responsible for you; whether that is in a good way or a bad way is also up to you.

Just as blaming removes our control over ourselves and our lives, it also doesn't allow us to correct our behavior or attitude since it presumes that these alterations are beyond our abilities. With a blamee (other than ourselves) identified, we can avoid making any valuable changes to our behavior or attitude. The author Aldous Huxley wrote, "There is only one corner of the universe you can be certain of improving, and that's your own self."

When you quit blaming you will be less depressed, less anxious, and less pessimistic. But, even better than that, once you take responsibility for yourself, you will be *happier*, more *optimistic*, more *cheerful*, and more *relaxed*. Happier people are more creative, more innovative, and live longer and healthier.

Achieve your potential

To strive for greatness and yet blame others for your lack of progress claiming that you don't have control over your destiny is futile. No matter how hard you pretend to want success, you are begging for failure.

Limiting your playing of the Blame Game helps you control your fear of success by being able to honestly appraise your own achievements and accomplishments; eliminating excuses for your lack of success and allowing you to thank others for their honest advice and feedback regarding your own irrational, self-destructive thoughts and actions. You will develop an honest and realistic self-assessment, in the absence of the guilt that derives from blame. This positive focus permits you to strive toward your goals.

Buddha asserted, "All that we are is the result of what we have thought. The mind is everything. What we think, we become." When we believe that our disposition is controlled by external factors and that we are not in control of our own future, and when we believe that making changes in our behaviors or attitudes is futile, we severely limit our ability to achieve our potential.

The philosopher Soren Kierkegaard wrote, "If I were to wish for anything, I should not wish for wealth and power, but for the passionate sense of the potential, for the eye which, ever young and ardent, sees the possible... what wine is so sparkling, so fragrant, so intoxicating, as possibility!"

We are all destined for greatness! We all have the power to achieve amazing things! Within each of us is an incredible potential! As the great statesman and inventor Benjamin Franklin stated, "The U.S. Constitution doesn't guarantee happiness, only the pursuit of it. You have to catch up with it yourself." When you quit blaming, you open your mind and thoughts to a high-energy positive potential.

Enhance Relationships

Being accountable for your actions shows internal strength and fortitude. It allows others to look to you as a responsible individual, which is an important first step to growing relationships. In 1990, Drs. Peter Salovey and John L. Mayer introduced the concept of Emotional Intelligence. In 1995, Dr. Daniel Goleman transformed the concept into a bestselling book called *Emotional Intelligence*. Emotional intelligence (EI) is the ability to reason about emotions and to use emotions to enhance our thinking. Dr. Goleman discusses the importance of impulse control and motivation in positive interpersonal relationships. In a review article about EI (*Annual Review of Psychology*, 2008), Dr. Mayer shows us that higher EI scores correlate with higher self-esteem, more satisfaction in life, and less depression. While these qualities seem intrapersonal, Dr. Mayer also describes how people with higher EI are better able to avoid arguments and successfully resolve conflicts with lower levels of aggression and interpersonal violence. Thus, your EI is also an important factor in terms of interpersonal relationships.

The better you feel about yourself, the better you are at maintaining successful relationships and the more likely you are to be judged as someone with whom a relationship would be a fulfilling. Is your EI score fixed in stone? No. Just like any other kind of intelligence, we can learn how to control and regulate our emotional state and become more intellectually aware of the impact that our emotions and EI have on intrapersonal and interpersonal relationships.

Improve your marriage

Like all of our other relationships, marriages are built on the positive values of respect and trust; in addition to other important positive virtues of friendship, love, and compassion. Blaming inhibits closeness between individuals and distracts from productive communication.

When we eliminate blaming from our marital relationships, we elevate that bond to a higher plane. The lack of blaming is a strong sign of respect and an indication of a strong connection between partners. Quitting the marital blame game is also an indication that you have amazing internal strength. Such strength is vital to allowing individuals to grow within their relationship. Successful marriages involve two strong people being stronger together. The positive communication, attitude, and behavior that results from the lack of blaming will transform your marriage into the kind only seen in fairy tales.

Make new friends

As you reduce your blaming time, your whole persona will change. You will take on a positive glow that will attract total strangers. This may sound unlikely but there is truth to these words. Positivity breeds positivity. Scientific studies that show how positive, happy, and optimistic people are more likely to attract others.

You can spend time with someone who blames others claiming that they aren't responsible for themselves, or spend time with someone who is confident and responsible. What will you choose? We have a desire to hang around people with abundant energy, especially if they compliment rather than blame. It's exciting and invigorating, even if you don't know that person. You can see it in their faces; people will see it in your face. They will want to be around you. Learn your secrets.

As discussed earlier, the less you blame the happier you'll be. Research has also definitively shown that happier people are more altruistic; more likely to help strangers. When you stop blaming, not only will strangers seek you out because you exude positivity, but you will have a greater propensity to seek out strangers.

Greater Success in business

Success in business depends on aptitude, motivation, and optimism. After we quit blaming and take on more responsibility for ourselves, we become more motivated to effect changes that we are able to control. We become more positive and optimistic as we realize the power that we possess over our daily lives. This may surprise you, but even aptitude will be improved when you stop blaming. How can this happen? Less blaming is associated with decreased anxiety and stress and more creativity and innovation. The combination of these factors allows us to reduce our inhibitions, to bring more mindfulness to our jobs.

Bosses want accountable employees. Workers want to work alongside those who are responsible for their actions. The positive attitude and reduced stress that is derived from quitting the Blame Game is reflected in increased creativity, personal innovation, and personal initiative; all factors crucial to entrepreneurial success.

Finally, as will be discussed below, when you exit the blame train, the increased physical health that accompanies your new-found responsibility will mean decreased sick days and absenteeism; two factors important in job retention as well as job promotions.

Gain respect

We allow ourselves, but not others, to forget things; we acknowledge that we are not mind-readers, yet we expect others to be. We expect others to be perfect and when they are not, we complain and are disappointed. These thoughts are critical first steps in developing an unhealthy disrespect for others. I had trouble getting where I needed to go because they drove too quickly or they drove too slowly; I couldn't do what I needed to do because they were too big or too small; I didn't understand them because they spoke too loud or too quiet. How can we respect people like that!

When we demonstrate our disrespect for others by blaming them, we push everyone away and we inhibit productive forms of communication. When we blame others, we claim to have little or no control over events that befall us and thus we show those around us that we are weak.

Quit blaming and take responsibility. This is the best indication to your friends, significant others, neighbors, family, and coworkers that you are someone who has something important to offer. You have seen the light and will share it with those near you. When people observe something "bad" happening to you and see how you respond by looking for solutions rather than wasting time blaming, you will immediately gain their respect.

When you combine the no-blaming benefits of increased happiness, optimism, and a positive attitude with improved relationships, a strong marriage, greater success in business, and achieving *and* actualizing your potential you can't help but gain the respect from those around you. Even those who are afraid of success want to be around those who are not. It's like getting an energy boost. It feels great to interact with someone who acknowledges their responsibility in a healthy fashion. People will also trust you to not talk about them or blame them behind their back.

Better Physical Health

Blaming obviously represents negative thoughts. In the extreme, negative thoughts lead to hypertension, ulcers, back pain, neck pain, tension headaches, depression, colonic disturbances, and dysmennorhea. Chronic high blood pressure in the presence of preexisting heart disease may result in heart attacks, strokes, heart failure, and, of course, death. None of these are good things.

So if we quit blaming, where will this get us? We will be physically healthier! We will reap the rewards of the infusion of positivity. Less emotional stress and anxiety will result in a reduction in blood pressure, myocardial ischemia (angina), and heart attacks. Research has shown that happy people are less likely to have heart problems and those that do have heart attacks are less likely to have recurrent problems. Improved thoughts, moods, and emotions lead to a reduction in ulcers and gastric issues, as well as fewer headaches, migraines, and back pain. This is not some New Age theory. This is science.

When you quit blaming, it makes sense that you will complain less when you get sick. You won't accuse your parents or your kids or your genetics or your clothing for your ills. It makes sense that optimistic people blame less. However, you will also not get as sick; your immune system will get a positive energy boost.

11. How to Stop Playing

"No one to blame! That was why most people led lives they hated, with people they hated. How wonderful to have someone to blame! How wonderful to live with one's nemesis! You may be miserable, but you feel forever in the right. You may be fragmented, but you feel absolved of all the blame for it. Take your life in your own hands, and what happens? A terrible thing: no one to blame."

Erica Jong

First, let me remind you that I still play the game. I'm trying to quit and have been moderately successful at weaning down my play time. However, without much forethought, I still find myself picking it up and playing a few rounds when I'm tired or feeling sorry for myself. The Blame Game is addictive.

Not playing the Blame Game doesn't mean that you should let yourself be taken advantage of or that you accept things that you have the ability to change. It also doesn't mean that you accept wrong actions or that you live with resignation. So, what does it mean? Not playing the Blame Game means that you concede that other people, things, and events do not have control over you. You accept control and responsibility for your thoughts, feelings, and actions—things that are under your control.

Implicit in this new-found power of control is that you may not be perfect and may, in some ways, need to change. Change is most often positive and what, on the surface, might seem to be failure, is actually an important step toward your success. To stop blaming means that you must judge others favorably. We do this by first empathizing, externalizing, and making excuses for others. Finally, try to view your problems as situations that you can explain, rather than complain and blame.

Acknowledge that you have control

"Control" implies not just having some ability to persuade, but dictating and exercising authoritative power over something or someone. When you want to turn on your TV, you may get up and walk over to it and push the power button. But more than likely, you pick up and use the remote CONTROL. Your TV has a control device and so do you. The reason that you've never seen your remote control is because it is internal. Only you have access to it. No one else in the world has the ability to use it, although we pretend that they can. Others have the ability to make suggestions to us, but they are only suggestions. This realization frees your mind to tap into a vast resource of power and self-control. You are not constrained or forced to do anything that you don't want to do.

Your boss tells you that you must work all weekend to complete a project. You have plans to spend the weekend with your family and you've promised your kids that you will take them to the movies on Saturday and then there's that Church function on Sunday and...

So, what to do? First, realize that you have several options. You can tell your family that you have to break your promises, do the work, blame your boss, and hate your life. You can talk to your boss, explain the situation and look for alternative solutions including the possibility of pushing back the deadline. You could also talk to your family and look for alternative times that might work out to get some work in. You could get up earlier or go to bed later and work when no one else is around. You could quit your job. That's right—I said quit the job! You say that you can't do that because you need the money and the security and there's too much debt and... Well, it is your choice to work. If you truly consider quitting your job as a possibility and you acknowledge that you do have this option, you will also realize that you and not your boss have the control. Your boss may phrase this request as a command, but it is really only a suggestion.

Whether it happens or not is your choice. Your four kids each made plans for this weekend to go for play-dates, music lessons, gymnastics classes, taekwondo lessons, and several different parties. You may be so overwhelmed that you agree to everything—one event at a time, one child at a time. You plan to figure out later how to actually make all this happen. You get a phone call from your second-best friend (your best friend, of course, being your spouse) who just came into town and are supposed to join for lunch. You're frustrated and blame your children for planning so many activities. You blame your spouse for being out of town on a business trip. You blame your friend for picking this weekend to come and visit. You blame your kids' friends for having parties. You blame God for only making twenty-four hours in a day. You're unhappy. You believe that your kids are controlling your life by making all these plans. But this isn't really the case.

You may have made promises to chauffeur your children to wherever they wanted to go and now that you have made these promises, you want to keep your word. But they were *your* promises. You had the right to decide whether you wanted to take them everywhere, or anywhere. This was your choice and under your control. Your kids have wants and desires but these weekend plans are not *needs*.

Making promises is analogous to handing over your remote. You are frustrated because you have unnecessarily given up your control. Make other transportation arrangements for them, cancel some of their social plans, cancel lunch or try to make other arrangements with your friend. Or, you can do it all and relax about doing it because you know that no one is "making" you. This knowledge will give you more peace of mind and perhaps remind you to not schedule so many things in the future. It may subtly push you toward occasionally saying no to your children when they schedule things, so that you don't later regret the decision and blame them. It's not their fault for asking, because they don't control your answer.

Take responsibility

You even control the things that you are sure that you don't. At the very least, you control your thoughts. Your thoughts precede your words, which precede your actions. I can't make you think anything or do anything that you don't want to.

Ken Keyes Jr. was a personal growth author and lecturer who had polio. He wrote, "You are not responsible for the programming you picked up in childhood. However, as an adult, you are 100 percent responsible for fixing it." In *Discovering the Secrets of Happiness*, Keyes described polio as a disguised blessing. He had every right to blame God or nature or his parents or the polio virus for his plight, but instead, he regarded it as a blessing, and this freed his mind, allowing him to move on with his life.

Only *you* can control what goes on inside you. You can often but not always change what goes on outside of you, but you absolutely have the ability to alter and improve how external events affect your thoughts and feelings.

Heritability alone does not determine outcome. You can be predisposed to become intelligent, but if you never read a book or become exposed to new information, you won't achieve your potential. It's up to you to make it happen. You can be "genetically predisposed" to develop arthritis, but how much discomfort you actually experience and what you do with this gift, is solely under your control.

Helen Keller was born in 1880; at nineteen months of age, she contracted an illness that left her blind and deaf. There was no standardized sign language or educational programs for those with disabilities. Did she spend her life in self-pity; blame her illness on her parents or God? No! Helen Keller became an accomplished author, women's rights advocate, the first deaf-blind person to attain a Bachelor of Arts degree, a founding member of the American Civil Liberties Union, and met every U.S. President from Grover Cleveland to Lyndon B. Johnson. She was friends with Alexander Graham Bell, Charlie Chaplin, and Mark Twain, and received the Presidential Medal of Freedom. She wrote, "Everything has its wonders, even darkness and silence, and I learn, whatever state I may be in, therein to be content." If you feel that life has been cruel to you and you can't control your destiny, write a complaint letter to the Helen Keller Foundation.

Implicit in your ability to control what you think and say is that you accept sole responsibility for your actions and mistakes. Learn from your mistakes, forgive yourself and move on with your life. Find the root cause of what you think are your *problems*, realize that they are actually just *challenges* and opportunities, and either try to change them to make them better or find a way to change your interpretation and feelings about them. Look at every situation as, "What could I do to make this better and what did I do to contribute to this."

Realize that failures are steps to success

Now that you have taken control of yourself and are the responsible party, this doesn't mean that you should be beating yourself up and walking around self-flagellating. Be patient with yourself (and others). The more you actively pursue control over your thoughts and feelings, the better you will become at doing it and the more of your power you will attain. Try not to blame yourself if you don't do something perfectly.

Appreciate that your failure is part of the process and part of the journey. Learn from it and don't get discouraged by it. You can use your mistakes and failures to discover more about yourself and how you best function. This gives you an opportunity to fine-tune your skills and develop in ways that you may never have dreamed of. This is a great process. What appear to be mistakes and failures are actually the first pavers on your road to success. We all know that nobody is perfect, but we often don't truly appreciate what this means for us as individuals. The river is constantly flowing and changing. Once you admit to yourself that you control your thoughts, you have given yourself freedom to change. Everything that you do, right or wrong, good or bad, will change you. How it changes you is only up to you! There is an Indian Proverb that states, "Blaming your faults on your nature does not change the nature of your faults."

Judge favorably

How can you stop blaming others for things that *are* under their control? Begin by using the general principle of favorable judging. Don't start each day with an imaginary target on your chest. People are not out to get you. Don't support the adage, "Just because I'm paranoid, doesn't mean that they're not after me." This is a depressing world-view and casts shadows of doubt on everyone that you interact with during the day. Get rid of this attitude and replace it with a general good faith in our fellow human beings. You cannot assume that others are operating on negative intentions and that only you (and maybe your mother) are "good-hearted" people. Everyone is essentially good. Start each day by providing everyone with a blank slate. This is the easy part. The difficult part is that when you assume that everyone is well-intentioned, someone will inevitably do something at sometime that you think is undesirable to you or for you. Now you have a choice—how to handle the situation. Immediately launch a Blatant Blame counterattack and go back to playing The Game, or judge favorably and go blameless. Yes, it is legal to go blameless in a public place. But how in the world can I not blame someone for doing this?

There are many fabulous mental techniques that can be employed in the act of judging favorably. Admit that you are not perfect. I know that most of you reading this do not think of your- selves as being perfect. However, when it comes to assigning fault or blaming, we often put ourselves on a pedestal. We rely on our faulty senses and draw quick and often incorrect conclusions. We often hurt others while doing this to try to protect ourselves. We don't realize that this doesn't protect us or make us stronger. This actually hurts us and makes us weaker. Every one of us has had episodes of mis-reading, mis-hearing, mis-seeing, and mistaking someone or something. We are absolutely positive that we heard or saw something that upset us, later to find out that it was not exactly who or what we thought it was. We thought that they were talking about us but they weren't. We thought they were talking about someone that we know, but they weren't. We thought they referred to our kids, but they didn't. We thought that they missed an appointment with us, but we had the wrong day or time or place. There are so many instances everyday where we jump to conclusions, fill in missing pieces, and assume we know when we don't.

Don't believe everything that you see, read, or hear especially if it appears to be something that makes you feel badly or something that you think is wrong, negative, or hurtful. Yehudis Samet in *The Other Side of the Story* has described multiple ways to judge favorably and give the benefit of the doubt. She encourages us to pretend that we are investigative reporters and that there is a missing piece of the puzzle. There is some untold story that we will, at some time, uncover. If we don't have the time or inclination to uncover it, then we can still assume that there is another explanation and now it's our job to make up a few plausible reasons that turn the story into a positive or at least a "neutral." Eliminate the need for blaming. Try to stay objective and appreciate how much we don't truly understand about what actually happened, especially about someone else's motivation.

How does this help? Maybe you never even meet the person who you are blaming. So why should we care? Maybe this is a Silent Blame that you keep to yourself. Why should this bother anyone else? Because it fills your head with non-productive negativity and restricts you from reaching your potential and achieving greatness. It needlessly shapes your opinion of that person as negative. That will come back to haunt you in terms of clouding your opinion of people in general, or you may interact with that specific person in the future and what could be a productive and positive relationship begins with flaws.

Challenge your perceptions, preconceptions, and your senses. Change your inclination from assume and accuse to excuse and explain. I was speaking with a friend who pointed out that she just received a "thank you" card from a couple that had come to a party at her house. She was somewhat annoyed and commented that the card came two months after the party. I asked if they were close friends and she said that they had been friends for many years and had done many activities together. I inquired whether she had ever been to a party at their house before and how quickly she would usually send off her thank you card. She stopped, looked embarrassed and said, "Oh my god. I never send them thank you cards. We've known them for so long. I think I owe them an apology."

In Judaism, there are 613 mitzvot that Jews must perform. Some people believe the word mitzvot to mean "good deeds," but it does not; mitzvot are commandments or obligations. One mitzvah is "In righteousness shall you judge your kinsman" (Leviticus 19:15). Judging favorably doesn't mean that you should not try to change things that can or should be changed. It doesn't mean that you should not make things better if you have the chance. It also doesn't mean that we pretend that everyone is always perfect and that anything and everything that people do to us is okay. It does mean that when something happens that you are not immediately happy about, take yourself out of the role of witness and put yourself into the role of judge – an impartial judge. Don't assume that you know the whole picture. Don't assume that you know what's behind someone else's actions or intentions. Don't assume that actions and behavior reflect someone else's personality. Your choice is either to try to find the positive in situations that you are not able to influence, or resort to a default blame and assume the negative. The difference in how these positions lead you to feel about yourself and your life is amazing!

Empathize—externalize for others

Our tendency is to not blame ourselves for things that we believe we were "pressured into" or things "beyond our control." In other words, we externalize for ourselves by blaming things outside of our perceived power. We know we are good and kind people, so if we did something potentially harmful to others, we must have had an excellent reason. When others perform the exact same acts, we blame them by internalizing their motivation as a negative intention and bad character.

So to quit the Blame Game, externalize for others. This is reciprocity; a fundamental moral value where each party has both rights and duties. It is a basis for the modern concept of human rights. The "Golden Rule" of do unto others as you would have them do unto you, has ancient roots. Treat all people as you would like to be treated.

Hand-in-hand with the concept of externalization is the notion of empathizing—the ability to recognize and truly understand another's state of mind or emotions. It represents the capacity to put yourself in someone else's shoes. If you can't empathize *with* others, you will have a problem trying to externalize *for* others. True empathy helps us understand and anticipate others' behavior. In general, it is easier to empathize with people with whom we spend a lot of time or those with whom we share many similarities. Like externalizing, empathizing is a skill that can be improved throughout one's life. When you, too, try to understand and appreciate someone else's actions in the framework of externalization, you can then empathize based on what you've inferred of their emotional state.

When someone does something that you don't like or something that you feel negatively affects your life, externalize their behavior—come up with some reasons, besides negative personality traits, why they would have acted in that way. Now empathize with them. How would you feel, doing the same thing to someone else? When you are able to truly empathize after externalizing, then you will have a hard time being mad at them and blaming them.

Make excuses for others

Every day we make excuses for ourselves while playing the Blame Game. How many times each day do you do something that you would be perturbed at others for doing? Driving too slowly, driving too quickly, talking on the cell phone while driving, speaking too loudly, allowing ourselves to be interrupted by our kids while we are involved in a conversation, moving in front of someone in line at the grocery store, leaving your cart in line at the grocery store while you go get one more item, etc. I know that you can come up with several hundred thousand more examples.

We make excuses for ourselves when we fail to accomplish a task or take on a challenge. We advertise our physical limitations, headaches, stiff joints and arthritis, back pain, short legs, bad memory, flat feet, sore knees, and weak ankles. We have lots of reasons for not succeeding at anything. We can say to ourselves, "I didn't see the light change to green." But when someone ahead of us doesn't go immediately when the light turns green, we say, "That inconsiderate dim bulb. Is he always that stupid or is he just making a special effort today. Why isn't he paying attention to the road? He's probably on his cell phone. He's a danger to everyone because he doesn't care!" Try to give the other person the benefit of the doubt. Make excuses for them. Make up the same excuses that you would have made up if and when you do the same thing. Perhaps the person who "done you wrong" and was destined to be your target of blame just had a death in the family, a spouse leave them, a new diagnosis of cancer or a brain tumor. All of these are possible. Perhaps they did something that seems very irrational. Is it possible that they do have some kind of brain tumor or mental disease that caused them to act in a way that is not typical of their normal behavior?

The Hebrew term *Limud Zechut* refers to looking for extenuating circumstances and trying to find excuses for others. Find merit in places that it might not ordinarily be found. Place yourself in their shoes and empathize with them. There's an old saying that states, "Don't criticize anyone until you have walked a mile in their shoes." That way, when you openly criticize them, you are not only a mile away, but you now have their shoes. Similarly, many people dream about success. We may fantasize about being famous and not truly appreciate that the reality for a celebrity may not be as glamorous as what it seems. In accordance with this, comedian and radio personality Fred Allen stated, "A celebrity is a person who works hard all his life to become well known, then wears dark glasses to avoid being recognized."

The process of excusing others begins when you suspect someone of doing something wrong, bad, or inappropriate. Instead of jumping immediately to blame, come up with several possible reasons why the person did or failed to do something that you would have liked. Pretend that it was you who did the same thing. How would you have excused your own behavior if you had committed the same act?

Somebody cuts you off by going through a traffic light which has just turned red and causes you to jam on your brakes. You've done this before to someone else. Did you do it because you're a mean and inconsiderate person? No, you had good reasons for doing it. You were late for the most important meeting of your life. You just received a phone call that your daughter was sick and needed to be picked up from school. You had bad news about an illness or death in the family and were so upset that you didn't even notice the light just turned red. These are just a few of the possible excuses that you can assign to the other driver. You are waiting for your friend at an appointment and they don't show up. You've waited long enough and are now very upset because they were so in- considerate and you took time out of your busy day. Stop! Think, have I ever missed an appointment that I really wanted to go to? Did you have the wrong time, wrong day, or wrong place on your schedule? How about the right time, right day, and right place but the time had changed from daylight savings (changed everywhere but on your watch). Perhaps you got detained with urgent personal or business matters that were unavoidable and your cell phone was out of power. These are real situations that happen to us and they can also happen to our friends, family, coworkers, and even strangers.

Once you have provided an excuse for them, try to believe it. Don't just mouth the words. Really make it true! You will immediately find yourself relax a bit. Tension will ease and you'll start a wonderful healing process. When you go through the large list of possible reasons for their actions, you will realize that there was a really good chance that they did have a reasonable explanation for their behavior. They did not disappoint you because they were mean, nasty and inconsiderate. What started as anxiety, stress, and apprehension from the incident, would normally progress to frustration, anger, and blame. However, now your slowness to judge, externalizing, empathizing, and development of excuses causes all that aggression to dissipate into understanding and relaxation and repose. You can't successfully accomplish this transformation and not feel better about other people. This feeling will translate into feeling better about yourself and life in general.

I'm not saying that everything is your fault and you should take the blame for everything. Understand what it is that you can control and be responsible for your decisions. There may be the rare times when you may truly not be at fault. Your accusations and blaming of a third party may be completely legitimate. However, simply the act of blaming ourselves or others suppresses our creativity and positivity. It negatively reflects on people in general and certain persons specifically and will eventually adversely affect your own sense of self-worth.

Explain, don't complain

The more that we try to truly understand other people, the more we are able to externalize their motivations and come up with viable excuses for their actions. The deeper our understanding is about any given topic, the more that we realize that answers and solutions are not so simple. Things are not so black and white. The more we can understand and explain, the less we will condemn and complain. When asked about her role in the American Embassy killings in Benghazi, Libya, then Secretary of State, Hillary Clinton responded, "What difference does it make at this point?" The difference is a matter of national security and the future safety of all Americans abroad, especially those serving our country as Ambassadors. When it is for safety, satisfaction, or efficiency, attributing cause is a meaningful and useful pursuit. Moving beyond blame and focusing on root cause analyses is necessary to improve dangerous system flaws. But this requires those involved taking responsibility – no thank you Hillary!

Motivational speaker and bestselling author of *The Energy Bus*, Jon Gordon, has also written a rule-book, *The No Complaining Rule: Positive Ways to Deal with Negativity at Work*. This one rule is so important that we are adopting it at our hospital. Mr. Gordon focuses on turning negative, toxic complaining into positive, productive solutions. In brief, "The No Complaining Rule" states that you aren't allowed to mindlessly complain to anyone who cannot help solve the problem. Bring the issue to someone who can effect change and have the complaint accompanied by one or two potential solutions (you can find more details at www.NoComplainingRule.com.) In this way you create, not simply influence change. Just as we can fact-find and attribute cause to work toward better outcomes without personally blaming, we can also discuss issues and look for positive solutions without mindlessly complaining.

About fifteen years ago after suffering from joint pain and swelling in my hands, feet, shoulders, hips, and back, I was diagnosed with psoriatic arthritis. I was devastated, and then bedridden and depressed for about one month. After several different types of treatments, my rheumatologist was able to come up with a successful combination of steroids, non-steroidal anti-inflammatory drugs, and the chemotherapeutic agent methotrexate. I slowly recovered, and after some physical therapy was able to start functioning at my job again. During the next few years there were some brief relapses during which I would go back on medications. Now after more than a decade, I am doing great! I could have chosen to play the "why me?" card and blamed God and my parents for causing or allowing my genetic predisposition to this illness. Where would this have taken me—farther down the path of feeling sorry for myself? Instead, I spent my time more productively understanding the disease process and learning the best way for my body to deal with this new situation. Today I feel great about my physical condition and have no one and no thing to blame.

By focusing on explaining rather than complaining, I am more open to alternative solutions and possibilities for improving my situation. *Complaining* assumes that you view this situation as a negative and a problem; and a negative situation often requires blame. On the other hand, *explaining* implies an open mind and a situation that requires a solution, not a blame. A solution is a productive, positive way of treating the situation. What, on the surface, appeared to be dreadful is actually a blessing in disguise. You would never have realized this if you were busy blaming someone or something for this awful incident that befell you. Explaining means looking for reasons and solutions. Implicit in the act of complaining is the assumption that there are no great reasons or solutions. If you are able to explain not just what happened but why it might have happened, you will open an exciting world of possibilities that starts you on the pathway to discovering that what seems bad is not necessarily so.

It takes twenty-one days to develop a habit. Rev. Will Bowen has used this information to initiate a program designed to help people become habitual non-complainers. As described in his book, *A Complaint Free World,* participants wear purple bracelets and move them from one wrist to the other if they catch themselves complaining. The presence of and changing of the bracelets is a frequent reminder to try to halt complaining habits. What occurs while people are mindlessly complaining? Blaming! Yes, the process of complaining is intimately and inherently associated with blaming. It is impossible to complain without blaming something or someone. So stop complaining and start explaining.

Believe in something

There are going to be many times when you don't have an explanation for what happened or why it happened. It may have been an "act of God." So, isn't it simpler just to blame God and get on with your life? While this is certainly possible and often occurs, the result is that your faith is destroyed and you are in the same situation that you were in earlier. Whether you believe in God or not, I encourage you to believe in something. Believe in nature. Believe in yin and yang. Believe in a universal, sustaining life force. Believe in Hindu deities or Native American gods. Believe that the journey is well worth traveling, making life well worth living. The journey is why we're here. For purposes of throwing away your copy of the Blame Game (figurative copy of the Blame Game, not this book, of course), believe that you have some kind of purpose in this life. Reconciling the existence of suffering with a belief in God is based on a combination of trust and understanding. Rabbi Harold Kushner has spent a great deal of time indirectly dealing with the issue of blaming. Focusing his efforts on why bad things happen, he has postulated that while God created the universe, and has a good and loving nature, he has, in essence, stepped back and no longer has complete control over everything that happens. Thus, bad things are more or less random events.

The presence of a semi-potent God may not be in accordance

with your worldview. If you put your faith in an *omni*potent, *omni*present, *omni*scient, and *omni*benevolent power, then you can have faith in knowing that somehow, everything that happens to you is for some greater good that you may or may not understand. If you believe that God controls all, then you should stop blaming immediately because everything that ever happens to you has been predetermined by God and is under God's control. Thus, blaming someone or something for your suffering is completely misdirected. You should be thanking them for all that they do to you and for you, since they are merely carrying out God's plan.

Suppose you believe that there is a God/creator and that he or she has given us free will. As a believer, you must still have faith that things will work out well for you in the end. Inherent in this belief is that while we retain free will and all of our actions are not micro-managed, God has an overall plan for the world. There is faith that we will end up in a good place; the journey that we take is up to us. So stop blaming God. Your path is under your control. In the Christian faith, this involves salvation and heaven after death. Implicit in this belief is that there is some purpose to my suffering—it is not random or meaningless. Labor pains would be less bearable (with a concomitant increase in the potential for blame) if not for the incredible purpose of giving birth. When my wife turned to me during childbirth and blamed me for all the pain, grabbed my lower lip and pulled it tightly over my forehead, she was really thanking me because without labor there would be no child. The pain is worthwhile when the outcome is explainable and beautiful. Not knowing the outcome is more likely to yield complaints and blames.

This philosophical view is only superficially related to fatalistic thinking, wherein human beings are powerless to make changes or to control their personal destiny. This religious theology situates itself well to fully blaming God for anything that happens. Although if you concomitantly believe that God is omnibenevolent, then everything that happens would be for a good reason. Thus, rather than blaming God for everything bad that happens, it should be incumbent upon those with this belief that God should be thanked for everything that transpires and that nothing is really bad.

I am not trying to indoctrinate atheists and convince agnostics. I will try to convince you to have faith in something. I believe in belief. When you have faith and believe in something greater than yourself, then life has more meaning and purpose. When you have faith in something, you are more likely able to forgive yourself. As pastor and best-selling author Joel Osteen has said, "You may make some mistakes, but that doesn't make you a sinner. You've got the very nature of God on the inside of you." This point of view originating in the belief of God releases you, in part, from self-blame, and if you view others as also being with and of God, you should be able to have the same compassion and lack of blame towards them.

I am not saying that you should believe in God and that will solve all your problems. There are probably more stressful situations in the world because of people's belief in God (I don't blame God for this). However, finding something that you are comfortable believing in does provide you with solace and an understanding in which you can explain rather than blame.

One faith that may be God-less is the belief that we are here for the journey. We may not know where that journey will take us, but we can be steadfast in our belief that our life's purpose is to enjoy our journey, our personal voyage. Each of the challenges will be good for us because we will learn, develop, and grow from them. No matter how "bad" they seem on the surface, we will look at them with respect and understand that in the end, they will help us in our personal growth. The goal is not simply to reach the top of the mountain, but to enjoy the ascent.

Some of you reading this may be believers in the "law of attraction." This is an old law that has been revisited and revitalized by Rhonda Byrne as *The Secret*. If you truly have faith in The Secret, then you know how important it is not to blame anyone for anything. According to *The Secret*, you must deeply and thoroughly envision what you most want and you will get it. If you keep thinking of something negative, that negative thing will surely find you. Blaming begins as a negative thought. Based on these principles, if you don't achieve what you say you want, you only have yourself to blame. This is the same principle of attracting success with mind power as that described in *Creative Visualization* by Shakti Gawain. Negativity brings negatively. Blaming someone or something brings about more blame. The journey also involves the Buddhist concept of "being here now" and living in the moment. The first popular *Be Here Now* book that set the stage and helped open the consciousness of a nation was by Jewish psychologist turned Buddhist Baba Ram Dass.

Meeting Ram Dass in the early 1980s had a long-lasting and positive influence on my life and how I personally view the concept of "now." The Buddhist monk Thich Nat Hanh has spread the concept of mindfulness meditation and the quintessential importance of attaining inner peace, emotional awareness, and psychological flexibility by being aware and mindful of all of our actions. The more that you live in the here and now, the less you compare this moment and this coffee and this weather to what it was like in the past and how great it will be in the future. The belief in the power of mindfulness is more than a New Age fad. It represents a system to which we may fundamentally base our life skills, psyche, and behaviors. Dr. Jon Kabat-Zinn is the founding director of the Stress Reduction Clinic and the Center for Mindfulness at the Univ. of Massachusetts. He has successfully brought the power of mindfulness into many medical centers and treatment programs.

Every time that we compare the now to what we think it was or will be, the more depressed we become at how bad things are currently. In several books on mindfulness, bestselling author, artist, and Harvard psychology professor Dr. Ellen Langer has clearly de- lineated the advantages of having a mindful outlook on life, learning, and creativity. Dr. Langer uses an evidenced-based approach to show us that when we look at life with mindless beliefs and attitudes, we give up control. Whether we do this via mindless task- processing or through blaming, we end up in the same dark lonely room. In her book *On Becoming an Artist: Reinventing Yourself Through Mindful Creativity*, Dr. Langer refers to one of her scientific studies where she gave a questionnaire to participants asking how frequently they compare themselves with others in terms of such things as wealth, attractiveness, fitness, and personality. They were also given a questionnaire that investigated how often they express negative behaviors and attitudes. There was a strong correlation between those who frequently make comparisons (good or bad) and the expression of negativity. Participants who were less evaluative experienced (made fewer comparisons), blamed less and felt better about themselves. Dr. Langer has also applied these mindful concepts to health (*Counterclockwise: Mindful Health and the Power of Possibility*); learning (*The Power of Mindful Learning*); and work (*Mindfulness*).

Comparing is our first step to negative thinking. When you compare the now to the past and future; when you compare the present restaurant to the one you were at last year or the one you will go to next month; when you compare this wine to the best wine you've ever had, you will most often conclude that the now is not so great. You probably complained just as much then as you are now, and compared that time to something that you thought was better in the past or will be better in the future. It's always better in your mind. Fortunately you don't live there. You live in the world of reality where things happen now. Instead of enjoying them, we compare everything to the perfect. When they are not perfect, we need to find out why, which means that there is something or someone to BLAME!

One difficulty in discussing why "bad things" happen is the definition of "bad things." People often refer to "bad things" as unpleasant. While this may be true, unpleasant does not mean bad. Staying up late to study for exams while you are also trying to hold down a job can be very unpleasant and difficult. But how lucky you are to have employment and spending money. How lucky you are that your parents taught you the value of money and education. How lucky you have the opportunity and ability to learn. How lucky you are to be close to finishing your doctorate degree. How lucky you are to be able to make this work worthwhile by giving back to the community through counseling troubled teens.

This is an opportunity to give thanks, not to blame. Similarly, with a practicing belief in mindfulness, mistakes are neither good nor bad. Dr. Langer teaches us that mistakes provoke and promote mindfulness, in addition to opening previously undisclosed doors. In social psychological studies, Dr. Langer asked participants in two groups to draw a picture of an animal or write an essay, and subsequently "forced" them to make a mistake. A third group of participants were allowed to draw or write without interference. Subjects who were instructed to incorporate a mistake (in the first two groups) into the picture or into the essay (in contrast to being told that it was human to make a mistake), later reported the most enjoyment in the activity. In addition, the art and writing from these groups was preferred by judges, even compared to those who made no mistakes! Based on her studies, as well as her personal journey into the world of art, Dr. Langer does not tolerate mistakes, she welcomes them. So should we!

A coincidence?

If a belief in God, a god-like being, a life-sustaining energy or force, or the importance of a journey doesn't appeal to you, then maybe you can try to have faith in fate. I can almost guarantee that everyone reading this book has had a "wow, it's a small world" experience. I'm referring to the kind of overwhelming life experience that at first seems like a coincidence, and once you reflect upon the odds of it happening seems so much more special. It's the kind of event that makes you realize that somehow the world is not as big as you thought it was. Maybe there is something behind the scenes directing some of these life occurrences, because it is too weird to be just a coincidence. "Synchronicity" is a term coined by Swiss Psychologist Carl Jung to describe coincidences that are just too special to be just coincidences. Your gut tells you that this is something meaningful and particularly out of the ordinary realm of coincidences. Robert Hopcke is the author of the best-selling book *There Are No Accidents*. He describes the phenomenon of synchronicity as meaningful sequences of unusual, accidental events. There is something bigger in the world with which our inner selves or psyches are in touch.

In the early 1980s I spent a few months traveling by myself in

Europe. I met someone named David in a wine cellar in Salzburg, Austria. David was from Canada and lived in a town not too far from my home in Toronto. We spoke for a short time and then parted ways. He was headed east and I was headed west. A few weeks later I was sitting near the dock in Brindisi, Italy, waiting for a boat to Greece and I noticed a familiar figure sitting on the dock near me. It was David. We resumed our previous conversation, found out that we had a lot in common and traveled together for a few weeks in Greece. After about one week of traveling, we were getting off a boat on one of the smaller islands when suddenly a tall, young, bearded man who was also getting off the boat approached us and asked if we would mind if he looked for a hotel with us. We told him that would be fine. This new traveling companion, Keith, told us that he had just come to Greece from Israel where he had been visiting for six months. It turned out that Keith was from Canada and we let him know that we were both Canadians. Keith told us that he was from Ontario.

What a coincidence, David and I were both from Ontario. Keith was from Toronto. I was from Toronto and David was from London, Ontario. I asked Keith where in the city he was from and he said, "The middle of the city." I was from the North End. "Where in the middle?" I inquired. "From the Forest Hill area," he replied. "Where in the Forest Hill area?" I continued. "Near Bathurst and Eglinton," he said. "Where around Bathurst and Eglinton?" I persisted. "On Elm Ridge," he said. "What number Elm Ridge?" I finally asked. "Number forty-three," he answered slowly, looking at me now with a little nervousness. "You live next to my grandparents!" I exclaimed. "They live at number forty-one." He told me that he knew my grandparents well. It turned out that we had worked at the same camp, but missed each other by one year; he was dating my cousin and we had many friends in common. Was it just a coincidence that on this remote Greek island we met for the first time? Possibly.

I told my uncle this story and he relayed to me that he was in the Grand Caymans on vacation and was lying on the beach when he decided to go for a swim. In the water he met a gentleman with whom he struck up a conversation. The man that he met was from Toronto. They spoke about Toronto for a while and when my uncle delved further into where in the city this other fellow lived, they went through the same back and forth conversation that I had had with Keith. "Forest Hill," "Bathurst and Eglinton," "Elm Ridge," and "Number forty-one." This man, it turns out, was living in my uncle's old house (when he used to live with his parents - my grandparents)! Is this small street in Toronto just that popular? Coincidence? Possibly. These things happen to all of us throughout our lives. Maybe they are all coincidences. But maybe they are not. Maybe life is more exciting and meaningful than the occurrence of mere coincidences suggest.

You're going on a business trip to London. You've just left a meeting in New York and are not going to have much time to get to the airport. There is a big traffic jam and by the time you get to the airport, they won't let you on the airplane. You have to fly out the next day. You are furious. You blame the people at work for not ending the meeting earlier. You blame the people in the parking garage at work for not allowing you to get your car out faster. You blame the people in New York for not taking the subway. You blame those poor people who were involved in the traffic accident. You blame the airline for not letting you get on even though the plane had not taken off. You blame the business people in London for scheduling the meeting for tomorrow. You blame your wife for not being able to drive you to the airport and her boss for not being more approachable so that she could get part of the day off to drive you. You blame your parents for not talking you out of being a businessman and you blame your in-laws for living in New York and causing you to live in this city. It seems everyone is to blame but you. As businessman Robert Half has stated, "The search for someone to blame is always successful."

On your drive home from the airport, you hear on the radio that a plane bound for London was just the victim of a bomb scare and was turning around making an emergency landing in New York. Your first thought, "Thank God I didn't get on that plane." Now, do you go back to thank all those people that you just blamed for you not getting on that plane?

How often do things happen to us that we initially interpret as being bad and later reinterpret as being good? Several years ago I was practicing martial arts and training some students in padded weaponry. I was working out with one of my top students when I was struck in the eye and began having double vision out of that eye. I blamed myself for the incident because I was not following my own rules and wearing a helmet. The next morning I saw an ophthalmologist and found out that I had incurred a corneal laceration that would take a few days to resolve. While I was in the office, he noted something peculiar during the exam. He sent me upstairs to see another specialist who performed a series of tests and diagnosed me with glaucoma. This second eye doctor informed me of how lucky it was that I came in because I had already lost some vision from the glaucoma and would have lost more if I hadn't been diagnosed. I went back to my martial arts class and thanked the student that hit me. By hitting me in the eye, he actually saved my vision. Bad things may not always be bad things. It depends on how you look at it, and the final outcome.

We're not always aware of what the final outcome will be. So try to assume that things happen for the good and not just by coincidence. You will have fewer things and people to blame and will get to spend more time having people to thank.

12. Conclusions

"When you cease to exist, then who will you blame?"

Bob Dylan

When "uns" happen — unexpected, uncomfortable, unpleasant, unwanted, and untoward events occur in your life, you have a choice of making yourself feel in control and healthy or victimized and unhealthy. Feeling healthy doesn't mean that you can't ever be disappointed or frustrated. Certainly feeling briefly saddened is better for your psyche and for your relationships with others than are feelings of self-pity, depression, panic, and hatred. But still these emotions don't typically set you off in a direction of healing and improving the situation in a productive way.

We are a society entrenched in blame. It is pervasive from the time we are born to our deathbeds. We blame and accuse every chance we get. No one, no thing, and no concept is free from being a blame candidate. We blame out of fear and we blame out of anger. We blame those we love, those we hate, and those we don't even know. Hall of Fame Football coach Don Shula stated, "The superior man blames himself. The inferior man blames others." However, we typically blame ourselves to avoid being blamed by others or we blame ourselves at times when we know that it was out of our hands.

There are many reasons for blaming; however, the root cause of all of this blaming is to avoid, shift, or reduce our personal responsibility. When we play the Blame Game, we don't simply relinquish responsibility; we give up a valuable piece of ourselves; we surrender control over our actions and ultimately over our lives. I refer to this process as "going down in blames."

What begin as excuses, transform not-so-silently into blames that limit our ability to achieve the greatness of which we are all capable. Jean Paul Getty, the American Industrialist who in 1957 was named the richest living American by *Forbes* magazine, was quoted as saying, "A man may fail many times but he isn't a failure until he begins to blame somebody else." In 1990, management guru Steven Covey wrote an enormously successful book called *The 7 Habits of Highly Effective People*, which has positively affected many lives. In brief, Habit one deals with being proactive and taking responsibility in your life. Habit two is about personal leadership and having a goal. Habit three involves personal management and organizational skills. Habit four is the habit of interpersonal leadership through seeking mutually beneficial solutions and win/win situations. Habit five involves communication and the importance of both understanding and being empathetic to others. Habit six is about synergism. In other words, the whole is greater than the sum of the parts; or still in other words, one plus one equals three. Everyone's contribution is important. Habit seven is about knowing and growing your "self." Steven Covey has since come out with an eighth habit involving leadership and helping others. Notice that not one of the habits involved blaming. This was not an oversight. Blaming will not get you to the places in which Dr. Covey is trying to help you ascend.

So here's the great news. You don't have to keep playing The Game! Yes, there is a lifetime warranty, but that doesn't mean that you have to play The Game for the rest of your life. There are plenty of other exciting games in which you can involve yourself. But, you must start each of these "positive games" by accepting yourself as a valuable person. Your mother always said, "If you don't like yourself, how do expect anyone else to like you." Your mother was so smart! Even if you screw up and make some mistakes, learn from them and move on. Use these same rose-colored glasses when you look at others as well. It's much harder, although not impossible to blame people that you like and respect. Jack Handey, writer and former member of Saturday Night Live once said, "If you ever have to steal money from your kid, and later on he discovers it's gone, I think a good thing to do is to blame it on Santa Claus."

Of course, all hope is not lost. Even for those who blame, there is salvation in the process of forgiveness. Eileen Borris, in her book *Finding Forgiveness* wrote, "Forgiveness is an essential part of *our* healing, enabling us to release *our* anger, pain, and suffering. As we forgive and heal our emotional pain, we begin to experience the gift of inner peace." These thoughts are backed up by scientific studies done by forgiveness researchers. One such individual, Dr. Everett Worthington, has been researching forgiveness for almost twenty years.

In *The Power of Forgiving*, Dr. Worthington teaches us about the forgiveness paradox wherein the process of forgiveness for the purpose of others' well-being actually yields huge physical and mental health benefits for ourselves. These are the opposite of the effects of blaming. Worthington has shown that when subjects imagined granting forgiveness in a criminal scenario, they reduced both fear and anger, and increased pro-social and positive emotions of empathy and gratitude (*Journal of Experimental Social Psychology*, 2008). Granting forgiveness was also related to more stable heart rates (associated with greater cardiovascular health). Dr. Michael McCullough, another pre-eminent forgiveness psychologist, has found that the process of forgiving allows people to overcome the negative effects that conflict exuded on their relationships. McCullough found that increased forgiveness toward a transgressor was associated with greater psychological well-being; more life satisfaction, positive mood, and fewer physical symptoms (*Personality and Social Psychology Bulletin*, 2008). Forgiveness was also linked to well-being for people who were closer and more committed to their partners. In his recent book, *Beyond Revenge*, McCullough teaches us how forgiveness has had an evolutionary advantage leading to maintaining close relationships. When appreciating forgiveness in this manner (rather than viewing it as an antidote for revenge), we are more likely to be able to invoke this protective mechanism.

One of the grandfathers of the Forgiveness movement and the Founder of the Forgiveness Institute, Robert Enright, has written

Exploring Forgiveness, to delineate how and why people forgive each other. Dr. Enright and his wife have used the results from his research to teach children in violent neighborhoods in Northern Ireland and in inner city Milwaukee how to forgive. People who have followed his forgiveness teachings have been able to "reduce their depression, anger, and anxiety, and improve their self-esteem." Psychologically healthier adults will, in turn, pay it forward by becoming more productive citizens and forming healthier community relationships. Fortunately, these emotional and psychological health benefits are sustained.

The decision to quit playing the Blame Game is liberating. Your stress level will go down and your satisfaction with life will increase. You will be able to rely on yourself, which is a truly amazing feeling. It will begin your pathway toward self-reliance and self-esteem. You will be able to empty your file drawer of all the excuses and apologies as you embark on a journey of love, kindness, and positivity that will engulf your soul. You will infect those around you with the gifts of forgiveness, respect, and happiness. The decision to do this is completely up to you. If, however, you choose to continue to accuse others and relinquish your control...

    Don't………
        Blame………
            Me!

About the Author

Neil Farber is a certified expert in blaming. He has blamed and been blamed for substantial and circumstantial things throughout the world. He was asked to leave the academic blaming community when he only blamed himself for not being inducted into the Blaming Hall of Fame.

Neil attained his B.S. degree in Psychology from the Honors College at Arizona State University graduating with Summa Cum Laude, Phi Beta Kappa, and several other Latin terms. He completed doctorates in both research and medicine. Dr. Farber has been inducted into the Medical Honor Society and received many research and fellowship awards. He is currently an Associate Professor of Pediatrics, Pharmacology & Toxicology, and Anesthesiology, a practicing Pediatric Anesthesiologist, an adjunct faculty in Psychology, and a certified life coach. Dr. Farber is a member of the International Positive Psychology Association, the Well-Being Task Force and the Professional Issues Committee for the American Society of Anesthesiologists. He is a lecturer and researcher in positivity, mindfulness, and conflict management, and a regular contributor for Psychology Today's Happiness Section. Dr. Farber is involved in international medical missions for children in South America, Israel, Asia, Africa, and the Philippines. He is a high-ranking Martial Arts Master Instructor who enjoys spending time with his family. He is founder of The Action Board – the next generation in goal-setting tools. Although he has numerous scientific publications, this is his first non-medical book. His mother highly recommends it. A portion of the proceeds from all sales is donated to medical missions for children.

Contact: TheKeytoAchieve@gmail.com

Like us on Facebook: www.Facebook.com/TheActionBoard

Index

Abraham 3
accuse 5, 8, 11, 35, 38, 52, 75, 80, 82, 135, 143, 159, 162
ABCs 35
act of God 88, 91-92, 150
Adam and Eve 2-4
Albert Ellis 50
Afghanistan 20
anger 17, 22, 45, 53, 67-68, 90, 147, 159, 161, 162
assumptions 51, 53, 124, 125
atheists 23, 87, 94, 152
autism 24, 99
awfulizing 59
Bacon, Kevin 31, 85
Bathsheba 89
Ben-Shahar, Tal 54
Bennett, Arnold 45
Benghazi 22, 148
Berra, Yogi 86
Bertrand, Russell 12
Biden, Joe 20, 114
bin Laden, Osama 31
Blame Documentation Device 10
blame in other languages 7 - 8
BlameMaster 63, 68
Blame Stylist 68
blamee(s) 22, 28, 29, 60, 61, 68, 84, 122, 128, 131
Blamers Quarterly 10, 72
Blaming Hall of Fame 84, 163
blaming rate 67
blaming targets (see Targets of Blame)
Bloch, Robert 1
Brown, Scott 121
Bruce Almighty 90, 91
Buffet, Warren 120

Bush, George W. 20, 21, 27, 31, 115-119, 121
Bush, George, HW 31
campaign
 of blame 16
 political 29, 32, 66, 113, 114, 121
Carr, Allan 86
Carry, Jim 90
cavemen 4-6, 13
Christmas Day bombing 121
Claus, Santa 161
Clinton, Hillary 21, 22, 114, 115, 148
complain 9, 49, 50, 57, 76, 81, 90, 134, 135, 138, 148-150, 154
Congress 14, 19, 27-28, 32, 112, 113, 117-119
Cooper, Rabbi David 87
costs 6, 124
Covey, Dr. Steven 160
credit crisis 26-28
criticize 35, 56, 80, 119, 146
Cowell, Simon 24
Darfur 19
Dean, Howard 121
divorce 71, 72, 79
Dyer, Dr. Wayne 128
Dylan, Bob 159
Einstein, Albert 110
electoral college 112
emotional intelligence (EI) 132
empathy/empathize 76, 145, 161
Enright, Dr. Robert 161
Enron 32
excuses 2, 20, 35, 39, 44, 55, 56, 92, 97, 101, 104,

130, 131 138, 142, 148, 160, 162
expectations 45, 46, 52, 66
externalizing 51, 75, 138-39, 145, 147
Farrakhan, Louis 91
fault 1, 18, 23-25, 29, 30, 32, 35, 36, 45, 46, 48, 65, 66, 69-71, 76, 86, 125, 126, 128, 129, 139, 141, 142, 148
fictitious characters 107-110
forgive 4, 46, 47, 141, 152, 161-62
FOX News 114, 117
Franklin, Benjamin 132
friends
   blaming 8, 29, 34, 44, 47, 74, 77-78, 96, 103, 129, 139, 143
   learning from 41-44
   making 69,124,126, 128, 133
   playing 6, 8, 40,, 97, 130
fundamental attribution error 51
Gates, Bill 6, 24, 56
Getty, Jean Paul 160
Gibson, Mel 14
golden rule 145
Goleman, Dr. Daniel 132
Gordon, Jon 148
gorillas 36, 38, 41
gratitude (see thank)
Gruber, Dr. Jonathan 117-118
habit/habits 78, 97-99, 150, 160
Hannity, Sean 21
happy/happiness 38, 46, 47, 50, 103, 127, 132-135, 162, 144
health
   care 117, 118, 121
   emotional 130, 162
   general 39, 55, 106, 122
   mental 24, 130, 131,154,161
   physical 98,134,135, 148,155, 161

height 40, 98
Hepburn, Katherine 74
Holidays 87, 103, 104
Holocaust 24, 91
hormone 16, 17, 77, 98, 105
innate trait 35-36, 46, 84
Internal Revenue Service 118, 119
Int. Blaming Fed (IBF) 1, 9,10, 62, 67
Iraq 15, 16, 19, 117
Jones, Jenny 22
Jong, Erica 137
Judge 33,84,88, 113, 138,142-144, 147
judging 142, 144
Kabat-Zinn, Dr. Jon 153
Keller, Helen 140, 141
Keyes, Ken Jr. 140
Kierkegaard, Soren 131
Kushner, Rabbi Harold 38, 75, 90, 150
Langer, Ellen 153-155
lead blamer (LB) 9
Lee, Bruce 62
liability 1,32, 55-57, 59, 65, 92, 101
Limbaugh, Rush 21-23
limud zechut 146
Madoff, Bernie 120
management 21, 57, 80, 81, 160
marriage 77,79,100, 128, 132, 133, 135
Mayer, Dr. John L. 132
McCain, John 115, 116
McCullough, Dr. Michael 161
mental illness 22, 54, 107
mind
   altering 2
   blames 49, 72
   control 23
   mindfulness 134, 153-155
   mindless 148-150, 153
   open 149
   peace of 139

Index

misinterpretations 53
mitzvah/mitzvot 144
mortgage 26, 27, 58, 120
MSNBC 97, 114
National Office of Blamers 9
natural disaster 5, 92-95
nature 9, 16, 37, 45, 46, 52, 86, 93-96
nearsighted 98, 99, 104
negativity
  behaviors 42, 53, 55, 130, 154
  consequences 48, 58
  feelings/thoughts 9, 14, 49, 79, 159
  general 78, 126, 128, 143, 148, 153
Obama, Barack 15, 20, 22, 32, 114-119, 121
Obamacare 117, 118
obesity 13, 96, 97
Oklahoma City Federal Building 25
optimist/optimistic 59, 131, 133-136
O'Reilly, Bill 21
parents 3, 4, 24, 35-38, 41, 42, 56, 76, 77
positivity
  attitude/psychology 25, 46, 58, 129-136, 142-43, 148, 152, 154, 160
  behavior 41, 42, 48, 51, 84
Presidential debates 20, 29
Ram Dass 152
Rational Emotive Behavioral Ther. 50, 59
Reagan, Ronald 117
reality shows 20, 28
relationships
  family 39, 125
  general 16, 24, 30, 81, 123, 159
  negative 78, 79, 103, 116, 118
  positive 124, 128, 132-133, 143, 161, 162
religion 8, 85, 94, 108
responsibility
  attribute 2, 38, 40, 64, 88, 93, 95, 109, 113, 121

avoid (shift/deny) 1, 20, 26, 39, 41, 44, 45, 47, 59, 65, 70, 73, 74, 82, 88, 93, 96, 100, 118, 123, 129, 160
  general 32, 46, 55, 62-63, 66, 78, 79, 115, 134, 159
  Taking 13, 48-50, 56-57, 72, 74-75, 79, 87, 90, 94, 101, 109, 111, 113, 131, 134, 137, 140, 141, 148
revenge/revengeful 66, 71, 161
Rhodes, Randi 21
Rivers, Joan 76
root cause 45, 141, 148, 159
Salovey, Dr. Peter 132
Samet, Yehudis 143
scapegoat 55, 85, 122
Sebelius, Kathleen 118
Security 14, 22, 27, 81, 115, 117, 138, 148
Seeger, Pete 123
Shula, Don 159
Singer, Isaac Bashevis 122
slavery 4, 13, 14
social pressure 42-43
Slender Man 108-110
stress
  enhancing 54, 57, 64, 77, 79, 152
  relief 50, 88, 134, 135, 146, 153, 162
Supreme Court 113
synchronicity 155
talk shows 20-22, 25, 26, 28
targets of Blame 14, 39, 62, 81, 84, 86, 93, 94, 101-103, 115, 120,

122, 146
taxes 13, 27, 115, 118, 120, 121, 123
Tennessee Williams 84
Thank (gratitude) 59, 87, 89, 95, 104, 106, 131, 143, 144, 148, 151, 155, 157, 158, 161
The Secret 153
Thich Nat Hanh 153
tornados 91, 92, 95, 102
Twin Towers 17, 25, 30
Types of Blame
   Autoblame 112
   Blamunition 40
   Blatant Blames 28, 61, 62, 66-68, 70, 71, 79, 80, 81, 107, 113, 114, 121, 142
   Blitz (see Secret)
   Brain Blame 82
   Bubbler (see Blatant)
   Burp (see Unintentional)
   Californian (see Deceitful)
   Casual 61, 62, 67-68, 78-80
   Chain of Blame 30-33, 62, 83
   Cough (see Unintentional)
   Deceitful 61, 62, 70-73, 81, 124
   Double-inclusive blame 2
   Group Blaming 4, 12, 17, 84, 85
   Hiccough (see Unintentional)
   Innocent (see Casual)
   Legal Blaming 29, 30
   Original 2, 88
   New Yorker (see Deceitful)
   Reflex 47, 63-65, 67
   Rubber Backing (see Deceitful)
   Secret 61, 68-70, 79, 80
   Slide (see Subtle)
   Spit (see Deceitful)
   Stealth (see Secret)
   Subtle 62, 65-68, 70, 77, 79, 80, 113, 114
   Unintentional 61-65, 67

Walkabout (see Casual)
Vietnam 19
Virginia Tech 23, 24
vitamins 130
weapons 20, 25, 31, 108, 117
What to Blame
   age 39, 47, 77, 106, 107, 109, 110
   body parts 106, 107
   cameras 44, 86, 106
   Canada 7, 85, 156
   cars 44, 86, 102, 106, 123
   Chronic Fatigue Syndrome 129
   earthquake 91, 94, 95
   genetics xii-xiv, 16, 46, 54, 77, 86, 96-100, 135, 149
   glasses 86, 99, 104
   God 2, 3, 32, 46, 49, 50, 52, 59, 86-95, 122, 126, 139, 140, 144, 149-152, 155
   guns 23, 24, 54, 55, 104, 107, 108
   inanimate objects 50, 104, 110, 123
   menstrual period 16, 105
   movies 23, 55, 103, 106-108, 138
   nature 37, 45, 46, 52, 53, 86, 93-97, 122-123, 140, 141
   Northern Ireland 17, 18, 26, 162
   pets 16, 101
   PMS 16, 17, 105
   Satan 93
   schools xiv, 21, 24, 25, 33, 35, 38, 40, 44, 53-56, 65, 69, 74, 81, 82, 100-102, 125
   Security and Exchange Commission 27
   skis 102
   smoking 42, 78, 97
   weather 38, 52, 95, 103, 153

Index

Who to Blame
  Americans 12, 17, 22, 25, 26
  African Americans 12
  borrowers 27
  bosses 38, 47, 57, 74, 79-81, 134, 138, 157
  children 3, 5, 15, 16, 34, 36, 38-44, 46-47, 55, 56, 72, 76, 77, 81, 84, 94, 99, 106, 109, 110, 139, 162
  Christians 4, 14
  Clinton, Bill 25, 31, 115, 116
  conservatives 21, 22, 26, 113-115
  coworkers 58, 68, 80, 83, 85, 135, 147
  democrats 18, 23, 24, 26, 27, 29, 111, 113-115, 117-119, 121
  friends 6, 8, 29, 34, 40-44, 47, 48, 58, 68, 69, 74, 75, 77-78, 84, 96, 103, 124, 126, 128-130, 135
  Greenspan, Alan 27
  homosexuals 12, 15, 16, 23
  Israel 14, 15, 17, 26, 31, 156
  Jews 4, 12, 14, 19, 25, 85, 144
  liberals 20-21, 23, 25-26, 43, 114-116, 119
  men 2, 13, 16, 17, 89, 100, 113
  Moore, Michael 85
  Muslim 2-4, 16, 17, 19, 23, 31, 85
  ourselves 39, 74-75, 131, 144, 148, 159
  parents 4, 24, 35, 38, 56, 76, 77, 98, 109, 135, 140, 149, 157
  Protestants 12, 18
  republicans 18, 20, 22, 26-27, 29, 111, 114, 115, 117, 119,
  siblings 4, 39-43, 47, 76, 77
  spouses 74, 78, 79
  strangers 1, 8, 9, 84-85, 102
  students 23-24, 74, 75, 81, 82
  teachers xiv, 36, 38, 74, 81, 82
  Tutsis 12
  victims 17, 22, 32, 85, 107, 123, 128, 129
  fictitious 107, 109
  women 3, 12, 15-17, 25, 105
  Wiesel, Elie 89
  Wilde, Oscar 61, 75
  Winfrey, Oprah 25
  World War I 12, 18
  World War II 12, 19, 90
  Worthington, Dr. Everett 161
  Wright, Rev. Jeremiah 32
  Writer's Strike 22
  Youngman, Henny 87

QUICK ORDER FORM:
The Blame Game

Email orders: TheKeytoAchieve@gmail.com

Please send the following books. I understand that I may return any of them for a full refund – for any reason.

- [ ] The Blame Game
- [ ] Making Lemonade
- [ ] The No Blaming Zone
- [ ] The Financial Industry's Guide to the No Blaming Zone

Please send more free information on:

- [ ] Other Literature   - [ ] Speaking/Seminars   - [ ] Consulting

Name: _____
Address: _____
City:_____ State:_____ Zip:_____
Telephone: _____
Email address: _____

Sales tax: Please add 5.7% for products shipped to Wisconsin addresses.

Shipping by air:
U.S. $4.00 for first book or disk and $2.00 for each additional product.
International: $9.00 for first book or disk, $5.00 for each additional product.

Index

www.ingramcontent.com/pod-product-compliance
Lightning Source LLC
Chambersburg PA
CBHW061310110426
42742CB00012BA/2132